Essays Perspectives Opinions

M. Fethullah
GÜLEN

Essays Perspectives Opinions

M. Fethullah
GÜLEN

compiled by

The Light

Published by The Light, Inc.
26 Worlds Fair Dr.
Somerset, NJ 08873 USA
contact@thelightinc.com
www.thelightpublishing.com
ISBN 1-932099-80-8

Library of Congress Cataloging-in-Publication Data is available

Printed by
Mega Basım
Istanbul - TURKEY

October 2004

Table of Contents

Preface

An intellectual with a distinctive spiritual charisma, a prolific writer and poet, M. Fethullah Gülen has been an extremely effective and popular scholar of Islam for the last 3 decades. Many college and university students and graduates, as well as the general Turkish public, have been attracted to his message of tolerance and compassion through education and self-improvement. His efforts to achieve this lofty goal, which had its humble beginnings in Turkey, now spans the globe and includes people from many different walks of life.

The foundation of his message consists of joining religious belief and modern scientific education to create a better world, one based on positive activism, altruism, interfaith and intercultural dialogue, and a desire to serve others and thereby gain God's good pleasure. Gülen has spent his career impressing on people that true religion preaches love, tolerance, open-mindedness, compassion, hard work, peace, and many other values and practices that lead a person to virtue and perfection. And, he believes, fusing the two types of education mentioned above enables a person to better understand the Creator's revelation of Himself to humanity.

The millions of people who believe in his ideas and goals have made themselves felt mainly in the fields of education and interfaith and intercultural dialogue activities through non-governmental organizations. Their activities have brought about hundreds of successful institutions, for Turkish businessmen have gone abroad in order to open and fund high schools, colleges, and universities in many countries with limited access to modern education and its resulting benefits. Other schools have been established in America and Europe.

This work presents Gülen through a short biography, a selection of various articles, his views on modern education and its importance, and how he has been presented in the media. It is by no means a comprehensive presentation of his life and influence upon millions of people; rather, it is meant to serve as an introduction to those who desire a better understanding of Gülen's message and what it has accomplished over the years.

Who is
M. Fethullah Gülen?

A Life Dedicated to Peace and Human Happiness

Introduction

Born in Erzurum, in eastern Turkey, in 1941, M. Fethullah Gülen is an Islamic scholar and thinker, and a prolific writer and poet. He was trained in the religious sciences by several celebrated Muslim scholars and spiritual masters. Gülen also studied the principles and theories of modern social and physical sciences. Based on his exceptional skills in learning and focused self-study, he soon surpassed his peers. In 1958, after attaining excellent examination results, he was awarded a state preacher's license, and was quickly promoted to a post in Izmir, Turkey's third largest province. It was here that Gülen started to crystallize his theme and expand his audience base. In his sermons and speeches he emphasized the pressing social issues of the times: his particular aim was to urge the younger generation to harmonize intellectual enlightenment with wise spirituality and a caring, humane activism.

Gülen did not restrict himself to teaching in the inner cities. He traveled around the provinces in Anatolia and lectured not only in mosques, but also at town meetings and corner coffee houses. This enabled him to reach a more representative cross-section of the population and to attract the attention of the academic community, especially the student body. The subject matter of his speeches, whether formal or informal, was not restricted explicitly to religious questions; he also talked about education, science, Darwinism, about the economy and social justice. It was the depth and quality of his speeches on such a wide range of topics that most impressed the academic community, and won their attention and respect.

Gülen retired from formal teaching duties in 1981, having inspired a whole generation of young students. His efforts, dating from the 1960s, especially in educational reform, have made him one of the best-known and respected figures in Turkey. From 1988 to 1991 he gave a series of sermons as preacher emeritus in some of the most famous mosques in major population centers, while continuing to deliver his message in the form of popular conferences, not only in Turkey, but also in Western Europe.

Main Ideas

In his speeches and writings Gülen envisions a twenty-first century in which we shall witness the birth of a spiritual dynamic that will revitalize long-dormant moral values; an age of tolerance, understanding, and international cooperation that will ultimately lead, through inter-cultural dialogue and a sharing of values, to a single, inclusive civilization. In the field of education, he has spearheaded the establishment of many charitable organizations to work for the welfare of the community, both within and without Turkey. He has inspired the use of mass media, notably television, to inform the public, of matters of pressing concern to them, individually and collectively.

Gülen believes the road to justice for all is dependent on the provision of an adequate and appropriate universal education. Only then will there be sufficient understanding and tolerance to secure respect for the rights of others. To this end, he has, over the years, encouraged the social elite and community leaders, powerful industrialists as well as small businessmen, to support quality education. With donations from these sources, educational trusts have been able to establish many schools, both in Turkey and abroad.

Gülen has stated that in the modern world the only way to get others to accept your ideas is by persuasion. He describes those who resort to force as being intellectually bankrupt; people will always demand freedom of choice in the way they run their affairs and in their expression of their spiritual and religious values. Democracy, Gülen argues, in spite of its many shortcomings, is now the only viable political system, and people should strive to modernize and consolidate democratic institutions in order to build a society where individual rights and freedoms are respected and protected, where equal opportunity for all is more than a dream.

Interfaith and Intercultural Activities
Since his retirement, Gülen has concentrated his efforts

on establishing a dialogue among the factions representing different ideologies, cultures, religions and nations. In 1999, his paper "The Necessity of Interfaith Dialogue" was presented to the Parliament of World's Religions in Cape Town, December 1-8. He maintains that "dialogue is a must" and that people, regardless of nation or political borders, have far more in common than they realize.

Given all of this, Gülen considers it both worthwhile and necessary for a sincere dialogue to be established in order to increase mutual understanding. To this end, he has helped to establish the Journalists and Writers Foundation (1994), whose activities to promote dialogue and tolerance among all strata of the society have been warmly welcomed by people from almost all walks of life. Again to this end, Gülen visits and receives leading figures, not only from among the Turkish population, but from all over the world. Pope John Paul II at the Vatican, the late John O'Connor, Archbishop of New York, Leon Levy, former president of The Anti-Defamation League are among many leading representatives of world religions with whom Gülen has met to discuss dialogue and take initiatives in this respect. In Turkey, the Vatican's Ambassador to Turkey, the Patriarch of the Turkish Orthodox Church, the Patriarch of the Turkish Armenian community, the Chief Rabbi of the Turkish Jewish community and many other leading figures in Turkey have frequently met with him, portraying an example of how sincere dialogue can be established between people of faith.

In his meeting with Pope John Paul II at the Vatican (1998), Gülen presented a proposal to take firm steps to stop the conflict in the Middle East via collaborative work on this soil, a place where all three religions originated. In his proposal, he also underlined the fact that science and religion are in fact two different aspects that emanate from the same truth: "Humankind from time to time has denied religion in the name of science and denied science in the name of religion, arguing that the two present conflicting views. All knowledge belongs to God and religion is from God. How then can the two be in conflict? To this end, our joint efforts directed at inter-religious dialogue can do much to improve understanding and tolerance among people."

Gülen released a press declaration renouncing the September 11th terrorist attacks on the USA, which he regarded as a great blow to world peace that unfairly tarnished the credit of believers: ". . . terror can never be used in the name of Islam or for the sake of any Islamic ends. A terrorist cannot be a Muslim and a Muslim cannot be a terrorist. A Muslim can only be the representative and symbol of peace, welfare, and prosperity."

Gülen's efforts for worldwide peace have been echoed at conferences and symposiums. "The Peaceful Heroes Symposium" (April 11-13, 2003) at the University of Texas, Austin, produced a list of peacemakers over 5,000 years of human history. Gülen was mentioned among contemporary heroes of peace, in a list which includes names such as Jesus, Buddha, Mohandas Gandhi, Martin Luther King, Jr., and Mother Teresa.

Gülen contributes to a number of journals and magazines. He writes the editorial page for several magazines. He writes the lead article for The Fountain, Yeni Ümit, Sızıntı, and Yağmur, leading popular and spiritual thought magazines in Turkey. He has written more than forty books, hundreds of articles, and recorded thousands of audio and videocassettes. He has delivered innumerable speeches on many social and religious issues. Some of his books-many of which have been bestsellers in Turkey -have been made available in English translations, such as, *Prophet Muhammad: Aspects of His Life, Questions and Answers about Faith, Pearls of Wisdom, Prophet Muhammad as Commander, Essentials of the Islamic Faith, Towards the Lost Paradise, Key Concepts in the Practice of Sufism.* A number have also been translated into German, Russian, Albanian, Japanese, Indonesian, and Spanish.

The educational trusts inspired by Gülen have established countless non-profit voluntary organizations-foundations and associations-in Turkey and abroad which support many scholarships.

Though a well-known public figure, Gülen has always shied away from involvement in formal politics. Gülen's admirers include leading journalists, academics, TV personalities, politicians, and Turkish and foreign state authorities. They see in him a true innovator and unique social reformer who practices what he preaches. They see him as a peace activist, an intellectual, a religious scholar, a mentor, author and poet, a great thinker and spiritual guide who has devoted his life to seeking the solutions for society's ills and spiritual needs. They see the movement he helped to nurture as a movement dedicated to education, but an education of the heart and soul as well as of the mind, aimed at reviving and invigorating the whole being to achieve competence and providing goods and services useful to others.

**Selected Articles by
M. Fethullah Gülen**

A Comparative Approach
to Islam and Democracy

Religion, particularly Islam, has become one of the most difficult subject areas to tackle in recent years. Contemporary culture, whether approached from the perspective of anthropology or theology, psychology or psychoanalysis, evaluates religion with empirical methods. On the one hand, religion is an inwardly experienced and felt phenomenon, one mostly related to life's permanent aspects. On the other, believers can see their religion as a philosophy, a set of rational principles, or mere mysticism. The difficulty increases in the case of Islam, for some Muslims and policy-makers consider and present it as a purely political, sociological, and economic ideology, rather than as a religion.

If we want to analyze religion, democracy, or any other system or philosophy accurately, we should focus on humanity and human life. From this perspective, religion in general and Islam in particular cannot be compared on the same basis with democracy or any other political, social, or economic system. Religion focuses primarily on the immutable aspects of life and existence, whereas political, social, and economic systems or ideologies concern only certain variable social aspects of our worldly life.

The aspects of life with which religion is primarily concerned are as valid today as they were at the dawn of humanity and will continue to be so in the future. Worldly systems change according to circumstances and so can be evaluated only according to their times. Belief in God, the hereafter, the prophets, the holy books, angels, and divine destiny have nothing to do with changing times. Likewise, worship and morality's universal and unchanging standards have little to do with time and worldly life.

Therefore, when comparing religion or Islam with democracy, we must remember that democracy is a system that is being continually developed and revised. It also varies according to the places and circumstances where it is practiced. On the other hand, religion has established immutable principles related to faith, worship and morality. Thus, only Islam's worldly aspects should be compared with democracy.

The main aim of Islam and its unchangeable dimensions affect its rules governing the changeable aspects of our lives. Islam does not propose a certain unchangeable form of government or attempt to shape it. Instead, Islam establishes fundamental principles that orient a government's general character, leaving it to the people to choose the type and form of government according to time and circumstances. If we approach the matter in this light and compare Islam with today's modern liberal democracy, we will better understand the position of Islam and democracy with respect to each other.

Democratic ideas stem from ancient times. Modern liberal democracy was born in the American (1776) and

French Revolutions (1789-99). In democratic societies, people govern themselves as opposed to being ruled by someone above. The individual has priority over the community in this type of political system, being free to determine how to live his or her own life. Individualism is not absolute, though. People achieve a better existence by living within a society and this requires that they adjust and limit their freedom according to the criteria of social life.

The Prophet says that all people are as equal as the teeth of a comb.[1] Islam does not discriminate based on race, color, age, nationality, or physical traits. The Prophet declared: "You are all from Adam, and Adam is from earth. O servants of God, be brothers [and sisters]."[2] Those who are born earlier have more wealth and power than others, or belong to certain families or ethnic groups have no inherent right to rule others.

Islam also upholds the following fundamental principles:

1. Power lies in truth, a repudiation of the common idea that truth relies upon power.

2. Justice and the rule of law are essential.

3. Freedom of belief and rights to life, personal property, reproduction, and health (both mental and physical) cannot be violated.

4. The privacy and immunity of individual life must be maintained.

5. No one can be convicted of a crime without evidence, or accused and punished for someone else's crime.

6. An advisory system of administration is essential.

All rights are equally important, and an individual's right cannot be sacrificed for society's sake. Islam considers a society to be composed of conscious individuals equipped with free will and having responsibility toward both themselves and others. Islam goes a step further by adding a cosmic dimension. It sees humanity as the "motor" of history, contrary to fatalistic approaches of some of the nineteenth century Western philosophies of history such as dialectical materialism and historicism.[3] Just as every individual's will and behavior determine the outcome of his or her life in this world and in the hereafter, a society's progress or decline is determined by the will, worldview, and lifestyle of its inhabitants. The Koran (13:11) says: "God will not change the state of a people unless they change themselves [with respect to their beliefs, worldview, and lifestyle]." In other words, each society holds the reins of its fate in its own hands. The prophetic tradition emphasizes this idea: "You will be ruled according to how you are."[4] This is the basic character and spirit of democracy, which does not conflict with any Islamic principle.

As Islam holds individuals and societies responsible for their own fate, people must be responsible for governing themselves. The Koran addresses society with such phrases as: "O people!" and "O believers!" The duties entrusted to modern democratic systems are those that Islam refers to society and classifies, in order of importance, as "absolutely necessary, relatively necessary, and commendable to carry out." The sacred text includes the following passages: "Establish, all of you, peace"

(2:208); "spend in the way of God and to the needy of the pure and good of what you have earned and of what We bring forth for you from earth" (2:267); "if some among your women are accused of indecency, you must have four witnesses [to prove it]" (4:15); "God commands you to give over the public trusts to the charge of those having the required qualities and to judge with justice when you judge between people" (4:58); "observe justice as witnesses respectful for God even if it is against yourselves, your parents and relatives" (4:135); "if they [your enemies] incline to peace [when you are at war], you also incline to it" (8:61); "if a corrupt, sinful one brings you news [about others], investigate it so that you should not strike a people without knowing" (49:6); "if two parties among the believers fight between themselves, reconcile them" (49:9). To sum up, the Qur'an addresses the whole community and assigns it almost all the duties entrusted to modern democratic systems.

People cooperate with one another by sharing these duties and establishing the essential foundations necessary to perform them. The government is composed of all of these foundations. Thus, Islam recommends a government based on a social contract. People elect the administrators and establish a council to debate common issues. Also, the society as a whole participates in auditing the administration. Especially during the rule of the first four caliphs (632-661), the fundamental principles of government mentioned above—including free election—were fully observed. The political system was transformed into a sultanate after the death of Ali, the fourth caliph, due to internal conflicts and to the global conditions at that time. Unlike under the caliphate, power in the sultanate was passed on through the sultan's family. However, even though free elections were no longer held, societies maintained other principles that are at the core of today's liberal democracy.

Islam is an inclusive religion. It is based on the belief in one God as the Creator, Lord, Sustainer, and Administrator of the universe. Islam is the religion of the whole universe. That is, the entire universe obeys the laws laid down by God, so everything in the universe is "Muslim" and obeys God by submitting to His laws. Even a person who refuses to believe in God or follows another religion has perforce to be a Muslim as far as his or her bodily existence is concerned. His or her entire life, from the embryonic stage to the body's dissolution into dust after death, every tissue of his or her muscles, and every limb of his or her body follows the course prescribed for each by God's law. Thus, in Islam, God, nature, and humanity are neither remote from each other nor are they alien to each other. It is God who makes Himself known to humanity through nature and humanity itself, and nature and humanity are two books (of creation) through each word of which God is known. This leads humankind to look upon everything as belonging to the same Lord, to whom it itself belongs, so that it regards nothing in the universe as alien. His sympathy, love, and service do not remain confined to the people of any particular race, color, or ethnicity. The Prophet summed this up with the command, "O servants of God, be brothers [and sisters]!"

A separate but equally important point is that Islam recognizes all religions previous to it. It accepts all the prophets and books sent to different peoples in different epochs of history. Not only does it accept them, but it also regards belief in them as an essential principle of being Muslim. By doing so, it acknowledges the basic unity of all religions. A Muslim is at the same time a true follower of Abraham, Moses, David, Jesus, and of all other Hebrew prophets. This belief explains why both Christians and Jews enjoyed their religious rights under the rule of Islamic governments throughout history.

The Islamic social system seeks to form a virtuous society and thereby gain God's approval. It recognizes right, not force, as the foundation of social life. Hostility is unacceptable. Relationships must be based on belief, love, mutual respect, assistance, and understanding instead of conflict and realization of personal interest. Social education encourages people to pursue lofty ideals and to strive for perfection, not just to run after their own desires. Right calls for unity, virtues bring mutual support and solidarity, and belief secures brotherhood and sisterhood. Encouraging the soul to attain perfection brings happiness in both worlds.

Democracy has developed over time. Just as it has gone through many different stages in the past, it will continue to evolve and to improve in the future. Along the way, it will be shaped into a more humane and just system, one based on righteousness and reality. If human beings are considered as a whole, without disregarding the spiritual dimension of their existence and their spiritual needs, and without forgetting that human life is not limited to this mortal life and that all people have a great craving for eternity, democracy could reach its peak of perfection and bring even more happiness to humanity. Islamic principles of equality, tolerance, and justice can help it do just that.

Endnotes:

This article originally appeared in *SAIS Review*, 21:2 (Summer–Fall 2001): 133-38. Reprinted with permission.

1   Abu Shuja' Shirawayh ibn Shahrdar al-Daylami, *Al-Firdaws bi-Ma'thur al-Khitab* (The Heavenly Garden Made Up of the Selections from the Prophet's Addresses) (Beirut: Dar al-Kutub al-'Ilmiya, 1986), 4:300.

2   For the second part of the hadith see the sections "Nikah" (marriage Contract) in Abu 'Abdullah Muhammad ibn Isma'il al-Bukhari, ed., *al-Jami' al-Sahih* (A Collection of the Prophet's Authentic Traditions) (Istanbul: al-Maktabat al-Islamiya, n.d.), ch. 45; "Birr wa Sila" (Goodness and Visiting the Relatives) in Imam Abu Husayn Muslim ibn Hajjaj, ed., *al-Jami' al-Sahih*, op. cit., ch. 23; and for the first part see "Tafsir" (The Qur'anic Commentary) and "Manaqib" (The Virtues of the Prophet and His Companions) in Abu 'Isa Muhammad ibn 'Isa al-Tirmidhi, *al-Jami' al-Sahih* (Beirut: Dar al Ihya al-Turath al-'Arabi, n.d.), chs. 49 and 74, respectively. The original text in Arabic does not include the word "sisters" in the command. However, the masculine form used refers to both men and women, as is the rule in many languages. An equivalent in English would be "mankind," which refers to both men and women. By saying "O servants of God," the Prophet also means women, because both men and women are equally servants of God.

3   See Karl R. Popper, *The Poverty of Historicism*, trans. Sabri Orman (Istanbul: Insan Yayinlari, 1985).

4   'Ala al-Din 'Ali al-Muttaqi al-Hindi, *Kanz al-'Ummal fi Sunan al-Aqwal wa al-Af'al* (A Treasure of the Laborers for the Sake of the Prophet's Sayings and Deeds) (Beirut: Mu'assasat al-Risala, 1985), 6:89.

At the Threshold of
a New Millennium

As every dawn, every sunrise, and every upcoming spring signifies a new beginning and hope, so does every new century and every new millennium. In this respect, within the wheels of time over which we have no control, humanity has always sought a new spark of life, a breath as fresh as the wind of dawn, and has hoped and desired to step into light from darkness as easily as crossing a threshold.

We can only speculate as to when the original man and woman appeared on Earth, which is equated with the Heavens due to the divine art it exhibits, its ontological meaning, and its value largely coming from its chief inhabitant: humanity. According to the calendar we use today, we are at the threshold of the third millennium after the birth of Jesus, upon him be peace. However, since time revolves and advances in a helicoidal relativity, there are different measures of time in the world. For example, according to the measure of time that currently enjoys global acceptance, the world is about to cross the threshold of a new thousand-year period. According to the Jewish calendar, we are already in the second half of the eighth millennium. Within the Hindu timeframe, we are living in the Kali Yuga era. If we follow the Muslim calendar, we are approaching the end of the first half of the second millennium.

We should remember, however, the fact that each measure of time is nothing more than a relative measurement. While a 100-year period is assumed to be the measure for a century, the idea of a 60-year century, based on the life span of an average person, is also worth mentioning. From this point of view, we are already in the fourth millennium after the birth of Jesus, upon him be peace, and third millennium after the *hijrah*, which is the starting point of the Muslim calendar. I bring up this issue due to the spiritual discomfort engendered by the terrifying auguries believed to be associated with the upcoming millennium, especially in the West.

People live in perpetual hope, and thus are children of hope. At the instant they lose their hope, they also lose their "fire" of life, no matter if their physical existence continues. Hope is directly proportional to having faith. Just as winter constitutes one-fourth of a year, so the periods in a person's or a society's life corresponding to winter are also small. The gears of Divine acts revolve around such comprehensive wisdom and merciful purposes that just as the circulation of night and day builds one's hope and revivifies one's spirit, and every new year comes with expectations of spring, and summer, so too the disastrous periods are short and followed by happy times in both an individual's life and a nation's history.

This circulation of the "Days of God," which is centered in Divine Wisdom, is neither a fear nor pessimism for those with faith, insight, and genuine perceptive faculties.

Rather, it is a source of continuous reflection, remembrance, and thanksgiving for those having an apprehensive heart, inner perception, and the ability to hear. Just as a day develops in the heart of night, and just as winter furnishes the womb in which spring grows, so one's life is purified, matures, and bears its expected fruits within this circulation. Also in this circulation, God-given human abilities become aptitudes and talents, sciences blossom like roses and weave technology in the workbench of time, and humanity gradually approaches its predestined end.

Having stated this general view, which is neither personal nor subjective but rather an objective fact of human history, it should not be thought that we welcome either winter or winter-like events that correspond to sorrow, disease, and disaster. Despite the general fact that disease eventually increases the body's resistance, strengthens the immune system, and drives medical progress, it is pathological and harmful. It is the same with terrestrial and celestial disasters. From a theological and moral point of view, they result from our sins and oppression, which are enough to shake the Earth and the Heavens, and from engaging in deeds that have been declared forbidden and despised by law and ethics (whether religious or secular). Even though they awaken people to their mistakes and negligence and provoke developments in geology, architecture, engineering, and related safety measures; even though they elevate the demolished belongings of believers to the level of charity, and the believers themselves to the level of martyrdom, these disasters cause much destruction and harm humanity.

In the same way, we read in the Qur'an: *Unless God hampered some (of you) with some other (of you), the mosques, monasteries, and synagogues in which God is worshipped would have fallen into ruins* (22:40). In other words, God would be so little known that men and women, who are inclined not to recognize anything superior to them and believe that their deeds will not be questioned in the Hereafter, would completely go astray, thereby making Earth unsuitable for human life. There is also the divine decree: *You consider something as evil although it is good for you; you also consider something else as good although it is bad for you* (2:126). For example, war is permissible. Although wars based on specific principles and with the intention of improving the existing situation may have benefits, they should not be demanded, since they bring harm; they leave behind ruined houses, destroyed families, and weeping orphans and widows.

Anyway, realities of life cannot be neglected, nor should they be ignored. Human beings are mirrors for God's Names and Attributes, and therefore are distinguished from the rest of creation with the honor of being responsible for making Earth prosperous in His name. If they cannot grasp the wisdom and purposes behind any good or evil that is sent their way by their Creator, they cannot escape despair and pessimism. For them, as is seen in the Existentialist literature, life turns into a meaningless process, existence into a purposeless vacuity, nonsense into the only criteria, suicide into a meritorious act, and death becomes the only inevitable reality.

The Basic Nature of Humanity

After presenting the issues that constitute the basis of this subject as an introduction, we can switch to our considerations regarding the third millennium.

Human history began with two people who constituted the essence of humanity and complemented each other. People lived a tranquil life during this time of the original mother and father and the families that descended from them. They were a united society that had the same views and shared the same environment and lives.

From that day on, the essence of humanity has remained unchanged, and it will remain so. The realities surrounding their lives, their physical structure, main characteristics, basic needs, place and time of birth and death, selection of parents and physique, innate characteristics, as well as the surrounding natural environment, have not changed. All of these require some essential and vital invariable realities and values. Thus, the development and alteration of life's secondary realities should be based on the axis of these primary realities and values, so that life will continue as a worldly paradise under the shadow of Heaven.

We mentioned above some issues that seem to be harmful and unpleasant. Similarly, there are human traits that seem to be evil at first glance, such as hatred, jealousy, enmity, the desire to dominate others, greed, rage, and egoism. A human being also has other innate drives and needs that allow the continuation of his or her worldly life, such as the need to eat and drink and the drives of lust and anger. All human drives, needs, and desires should be guided and trained in the direction of the eternal, universal, and invariable values that address the fundamental aspects of humanity. In this respect, the need to eat and drink, and the desire associated with lust and rage, can be tamed and transformed into means of absolute or relative good.

Likewise, egoism and hatred can become sources of fine attributes and goodness. Jealousy and rivalry can be transformed into competition in charitable and good deeds. The feeling of enmity can be transformed into enmity against Satan, the greatest enemy of humanity, and against the feeling of enmity itself and hatred. Greed and rage can force one to perform good deeds without tiredness. Egoism can point out the evil aspects of the carnal soul (*nafs*), thereby seeking to train and purify the soul by not excusing its evil actions.

All negative feelings can be transformed into sources of good by training and struggle. This is how one reaches the level of "the best of Creation," by traveling the way of transformation from a potential human being to a real and perfected human being, to becoming the best symbol, model, and personal representative of creation and existence.

Despite this fact, the realities of human life do not always follow these guidelines. Negative feelings and attributes often defeat people, pulling them under their domination to such an extent that even the religions that guide people to goodness and kindness are abused, as well as the feelings and attributes that are sources of absolute good. Human life, at the level of the individual and of humanity as a whole, is merely the summation of internal, personal struggles and their external manifestations. These tides make the personal world of the individual, society, and history an arena of battle, struggle, war, oppression, and tyranny. As a result, it is usually human beings themselves who suffer the consequences.

Men and women always receive the fruits of their deeds. In the first period of its history, humanity lived a happy life as a single society whose members shared their joys and sorrows. But, later on they bound their necks and feet with a rusty yoke composed of chains of oppression as a result of jealousy, greed, and coveting other's rights and properties. The consequence was Cain's murder of Abel. As a result of this, humanity entered the path of disunity. Despite the millenniums coming one after the other like days, seasons and years, this "cycle" still continues.

The Second Millennium

The second millennium started with the Crusades and then the Mongol invasions of the Muslim world, which was like the heart of Earth and history at that time. Despite the wars and destruction, and despite the crimes committed sometimes in the name of religion and sometimes in the name of economic, political, and military supremacy, this millennium has seen the apex of the East's civilizations, based on spirituality, metaphysical, universal, and eternal values, and the West's civilizations, based on the physical sciences. Many significant geographical discoveries and scientific inventions have occurred.

However, the East's and West's civilizations existed separated from each other. This separation, which should not have occurred, was based on the former's retiring from the intellect and science, while the latter retired from spirituality, metaphysics, and eternal and invariable values. As a result, the last centuries of this millennium have witnessed disasters that are hard to believe. Due to humanity's growing arrogance and egoism, arising from its accomplishments, men and women have had to live through worldwide colonialism, immense massacres, revolutions that cost millions of lives, unimaginably bloody and destructive wars, racial discrimination, immense social and economic injustice, and iron curtains built by regimes whose ideology and philosophy sought to deny the essence, freedom, merit, and honor of humanity. It is partly because of this and partly because of some auguries from the Bible that many people in the West fear that the world will again be soaked by floods of blood, pus, and destruction. They are quite pessimistic and worried about the new millennium.

Our Expectations

Modern means of communication and transportation have transformed the world into a large, global village. So, those who expect that any radical changes in a country will be determined by that country alone and remain limited to it are unaware of current realities. This time is a period of interactive relations. Nations and peoples are more in need of and dependent on each other, which causes closeness in mutual relations.

This network of relations, which has surpassed the period of brute colonialism and exists on the basis of mutual interest, provides some benefits to the weaker side. Moreover, owing to the advances in technology, especially digital electronic technology, the acquisition and exchange of information grows gradually. As a result, the individual comes to the fore, making it inevitable that democratic governments that respect personal rights will replace oppressive regimes.

As each individual is like a species with respect to other species, individual rights cannot be sacrificed for society, and social rights should depend on individual rights. This is why the basic human rights and freedoms found in the revealed religions came to be considered by a war-weary West. They will enjoy priority in all relations. At the head of these rights is the right to life, which is granted and can be taken only by God. To accentuate the importance of this right in Islam, a basic Qur'anic principle is that: *If one person kills another unjustly, it is the same as if he or she has killed all of humanity; if one saves another, it is the same as if he or she has saved all of humanity* (5:32).

Other rights are the freedom of religion and belief, thought and expression; the right to own property and the sanctity of one's home; to marry and have children; to communicate and travel; and the right to and freedom of education. The principles of Islamic jurisprudence are based on these and other rights, all of which are accepted by modern legal systems, such as the protection of life, religion, property, reproduction, and intellect, as well as equality of people based on the fact that all people are human beings, and the rejection of all racial, color, and linguistic discrimination. All of these will be—and should be—indispensable essentials in the new millennium.

I believe and hope that the world of the new millennium will be a happier, more just, and more compassionate place, contrary to the fears of some people. Islam, Christianity, and Judaism all come from the same root, have almost the same essentials, and are nourished from the same source. Although they have lived as rival religions for centuries, the common points between them and their shared responsibility to build a happy world for all of the creatures of God make interfaith dialogue among them necessary. This dialogue has now expanded to include the religions of Asia and other areas. The results have been positive.

As mentioned above, this dialogue will develop as a necessary process, and the followers of all religions will find ways to get closer and assist each other.

Previous generations witnessed a bitter struggle that should never have taken place: science versus religion. This conflict gave rise to atheism and materialism, which influenced Christianity more than other religions. Science cannot contradict religion, for its purpose is to understand nature and humanity, which are each a composition of the manifestations of God's Attributes of Will and Power. Religion has its source in the Divine Attribute of Speech, which was manifested in the course of human history as Divine Scriptures such as the Qur'an, the Gospels, the Torah and others. Thanks to the efforts of both Christian and Muslim theologians and scientists, it seems that the few-century-long religion–science conflict will come to an end, or at least its absurdity will be acknowledged.

The end of this conflict and a new style of education fusing religious and scientific knowledge with morality and spirituality will produce genuinely enlightened people with hearts illumined by religious sciences and spirituality, minds illuminated with positive sciences, characterized by all kinds of humane merits and moral values, and cognizant of the socioeconomic and political conditions of their time. Our old world will experience an excellent "springtime" before its demise. This springtime will see the gap between rich and poor narrow; the world's riches distributed most justly according to one's work, capital, and needs; the absence of discrimination based on race, color, language, and worldview; and basic human rights and freedoms protected. Individuals will come to the fore and, learning how to realize their potential, will ascend on the way to becoming "the most elevated human" with the wings of love, knowledge, and belief.

In this new springtime, when scientific and technological progress is taken into consideration, people will understand that the current level of science and technology resembles the stage when an infant is learning how to crawl. Humanity will organize trips into space as if traveling to another country. Travelers on the way to God, those self-immolators of love who have no time for hostility, will carry the inspirations in their spirits to other worlds.

Yes, this springtime will rise on the foundations of love, compassion, mercy, dialogue, acceptance of others, mutual respect, justice, and rights. It will be a time in which humanity will discover its real essence. Goodness and kindness, righteousness and virtue will form the basic essence of the world. No matter what happens, the world will come to this track sooner or later. Nobody can prevent this.

We pray and beg the Infinitely Compassionate One not to let our hopes and expectations come to nothing.

Endnote:

This article originally appeared in *The Fountain* 3:29 (Jan.–Mar. 2000): 7-8.

The Necessity
of Interfaith Dialogue

Introduction

Today, people are talking about many things: the danger of war and frequent clashes, water and air pollution, hunger, the increasing erosion of moral values, and so on. As a result, many other concerns have come to the fore: peace, contentment, ecology, justice, tolerance, and dialog. Unfortunately, despite certain promising precautions, those who should be tackling these problems tend to do so by seeking further ways to conquer and control nature and produce more lethal weapons. Obscene material is spread through the mass media, especially the Internet.

At the root of the problem is the materialist worldview, which severely limits religion's influence in contemporary social life. The result is the current disturbed balance between humanity and nature and within individual men and women. Only a few people seem to realize that social harmony and peace with nature, between people, and within the individual only can come about when the material and spiritual realms are reconciled. Peace with nature, peace and justice in society, and personal integrity are possible when one is at peace with Heaven.

Religion reconciles opposites that seem to be mutually exclusive: religion-science, this world-the next world, nature-Divine Books, the material-the spiritual, and spirit-body. Religion can erect a defense against the destruction caused by scientific materialism, put science in its proper place, and end long-standing conflicts among nations and peoples. The natural sciences, which should act as steps of light leading people to God, have become a cause of unbelief on a previously unknown scale. As the West has become the main base for this unbelief, and because Christianity has been the religion most influenced by it, dialog between Muslims and Christians appears to be indispensable.

The goal of dialog among world religions is not simply to destroy scientific materialism and the destructive materialistic worldview; rather, the very nature of religion demands this dialog. Judaism, Christianity, and Islam, and even Hinduism and other world religions accept the same source for themselves, and, including Buddhism, pursue the same goal. As a Muslim, I accept all Prophets and Books sent to different peoples throughout history, and regard belief in them as an essential principle of being Muslim. A Muslim is a true follower of Abraham, Moses, David, Jesus, and all other Prophets. Not believing in one Prophet or Book means that one is not a Muslim. Thus we acknowledge the oneness and basic unity of religion, which is a symphony of God's blessings and mercy, and the universality of belief in religion. So, religion is a system of belief embracing all races and all beliefs, a road bringing everyone together in brotherhood.

Regardless of how their adherents implement their faith in their daily lives, such generally accepted values as love, respect, tolerance, forgiveness, mercy, human rights, peace, brotherhood, and freedom exalted by religion. Most of them are accorded the highest precedence in the messages brought by Moses, Jesus, and Muhammad, as well as in the messages of Buddha and even Zarathustra, Lao-Tzu, Confucius, and the Hindu scholars.

We have a Prophetic Tradition almost unanimously recorded in the Hadith literature that Jesus will return when the end of the world is near. We do not know whether he will actually reappear physically, but what we understand is that near the end of time, values like love, peace, brotherhood, forgiveness, altruism, mercy, and spiritual purification will have precedence, as they did during Jesus' ministry. In addition, because Jesus was sent to the Jews and because all Hebrew Prophets exalted these values, it will be necessary to establish a dialog with the Jews as well as a closer relationship and co-operation among Islam, Christianity, and Judaism.

There are many common points for dialog among devout Muslims, Christians, and Jews. As pointed out by Michael Wyschogrod, an American professor of philosophy, there are just as many theoretical or creedal reasons for Muslims and Jews drawing closer to one another as there are for Jews and Christians coming together.[1] Furthermore, practically and historically, the Muslim world has a good record of dealing with the Jews: There has been almost no discrimination, and no Holocaust, denial of basic human rights, or genocide. On the contrary, Jews always have been welcomed in times of trouble, as when the Ottoman State embraced them after their expulsion from Andalusia (Spain).

Muslim Difficulties in Dialog

Christians, Jews, and others may face internal difficulties in dialog. I would like to make a brief survey of certain reasons why Muslims find it hard to establish dialog. The same reasons are responsible for the present misunderstanding of Islam.

According to Fuller and Lesser, in the last century alone far more Muslims have been killed by Western powers than all Christians killed by Muslims throughout history. [2] Many Muslims tend to produce more comprehensive results, and believe that Western policies are designed to weaken Muslim power. This historical experience leads even educated and conscious Muslims to believe that the West is continuing its 1,000-year-old systematic aggression against Islam and, even worse, with far more subtle and sophisticated methods. Consequently, the Church's call for dialog meets with considerable suspicion.

In addition, the Islamic world entered the twentieth century under the direct or indirect European domination. The Ottoman Empire, the defender and greatest representative of this world, collapsed as a result of European attacks. Turkey followed the Muslim peoples' struggles against foreign invasions with great interest. In addition to this, internal Turkish conflicts between the Democratic Party and People's Party in the 1950s led to Islam's being perceived by conservatives and some intellectuals as an ideology of conflict and reaction and a political system, rather than as a religion primarily addressing one's heart, spirit, and mind. Perceiving Islam as a party ideology in some Muslim countries, including Turkey, contributed to this impression. As a result, secularists and others began to look upon all Muslims and Islamic activities as suspect.

Islam also is seen as a political ideology, for it was the greatest dynamic in the Muslims' wars of independence. Thus it has become identified as an ideology of independence. Ideology tends to separate, while religion means enlightenment of the mind together with belief, contentment, and tranquility of the heart, sensitivity in conscience, and perception through real experience. By its very nature, religion penetrates such essential virtues as faith, love, mercy, and compassion. Reducing religion to a harsh political ideology and a mass ideology of independence has erected walls between Islam and the West, and has caused Islam to be misunderstood.

Christendom's historical portrayal of Islam also has weakened Muslims' courage with respect to interfaith dialog. For centuries, Christians were told that Islam was a crude and distorted version of Judaism and Christianity, and so the Prophet was considered an imposter, a common or ingenious trickster, the Antichrist, or an idol worshipped by Muslims. Even recent books have presented him as someone with strange ideas who believed he had to succeed at any cost, and who resorted to any means to achieve success.

Dialog Is a Must

Interfaith dialog is a must today, and the first step in establishing it is forgetting the past, ignoring polemical arguments, and giving precedence to common points, which far outnumber polemical ones. In the West, some attitudinal changes can be seen in some intellectuals and clerics toward Islam. I must particularly mention the late Massignon, who referred to Islam by the expression: "The faith of Abraham revived with Muhammad." He believed that Islam has a positive, almost prophetic mission in the post-Christian world, for: "Islam is the religion of faith. It is not a religion of natural faith in the God of the philosophers, but faith in the God of Abraham, of Isaac, and of Ishmael, faith in our God. Islam is a great mystery of Divine Will." He believed in the Divine authorship of the Qur'an and Muhammad's Prophethood.[3]

The West's perspective on our Prophet also has softened. Together with Christian clerics and men of religion, many Western thinkers besides Massignon, like Charles J. Ledit, Y. Moubarac, Irene-M. Dalmais, L. Gardet, Norman Daniel, Michel Lelong, H. Maurier, Olivier Lacombe, and Thomas Merton express warmth for both Islam and for our Prophet, and support the call for dialog.

Also, what the final declaration of the Second Vatican Council, which began the process of dialog, said about

Islam cannot be ignored. This means that the attitude of the Catholic Church toward Islam has now changed. In the second period of the Council, Pope Paul VI said:

> On the other hand, the Catholic Church is looking farther, beyond the horizons of Christianity. It is turning towards other religions that preserve the concept and meaning of God as One, Transcendental, Creator, Ruler of Fate and Wise. Those religions worship God with sincere, devotional actions.

He also indicated that the Catholic Church commended these religions' good, true, and humane sides:

> The Church reaffirms to them that in modern society in order to save the meaning of religion and servanthood to God-a necessity and need of true civilization-the Church itself is going to take its place as a resolute advocate of God's rights on man.

As a final result, the written statement entitled "A Declaration Regarding the Church's Relations with non-Christian Religions," which was accepted at the Council, declared that:

> In our world that has become smaller and in which relations have become closer, people are expecting answers from religion regarding mysterious enigmas in human nature that turn their hearts upside down. What is man? What is the meaning and purpose of life? What is goodness and reward, what is sin? What is the source and point of suffering? What is the path to true happiness? What is death, what is the meaning of judgement after death and receiving the fruits of what one has done on earth? What is the mystery surrounding the beginning and end of existence?

After stating that different religions attempt to answer these questions in their own ways, and that the Church does not reject altogether the values of other religions, the Council encourages Christians to have dialog with members of other religions:

> The Church encourages its children, together with believing and living as Christians, to get to know and support with precaution, compassion, dialog and co-operation those who follow other religions and to encourage them to develop their spiritual, moral and socio-cultural values.[4]

Another important point is that Pope John Paul II admits in his *Crossing the Threshold of Hope* that (despite Muslim neglect and carelessness), it is still the Muslims who worship in the best and most careful manner. He reminds his readers that, on this point, Christians should take Muslims as their example.

In addition, Islam's resistance to materialist ideologies and its important role in the modern world has amazed many Western observers. The observations of E. H. Jurji are very significant here:

> In its self-respect, self-maintenance, and realistic zeal, in its fight for solidarity against racist and Marxist ideologies, in its vigorous denunciation of exploitation, as in the preaching of its message to a wayward, bleeding humanity, Islam faces the modern world with a peculiar sense of mission. Not confused and not torn apart by a mass of theological subtleties, nor buried beneath a heavy burden of dogma, this sense of mission draws its strength from a complete conviction of the relevance of Islam.[5]

Muslims and the West have struggled with each other for almost 1,400 years. From the Western perspective, Islam has threatened and opened many Western doors, facts that have not been forgotten. That said, the fact that this struggle is leading Muslims to oppose and resent the West will never benefit Islam or Muslims. Modern transportation and mass communication have turned the world into a global village in which every relationship is interactive. The West cannot wipe out Islam or its territory, and Muslim armies can no longer march on the West.

Moreover, as this world is becoming even more global, both sides feel the need for a give-and-take relationship. The West has scientific, technological, economic, and military supremacy. However, Islam possesses more important and vital factors: Islam, as represented by the Qur'an and Sunna, has retained the freshness of its beliefs, spiritual essence, good works, and morality as it has unfolded over the last 14 centuries. In addition, it has the potential to blow spirit and life into Muslims, numbed for centuries, as well as into many other peoples drowned in the swamp of materialism.

Just as religion has not yet escaped the onslaught of unbelief based on science and philosophy, no one can guarantee that this storm will not blow even stronger in the future. These and other factors do not allow Muslims to view and present Islam purely as a political ideology or an economic system. Neither do they allow Muslims to consider the West, Christianity, Judaism, and even other great religions like Buddhism from a historical perspective and define their attitude accordingly.

When those who have adopted Islam as a political ideology, rather than a religion in its true sense and function, review their self-proclaimed Islamic activities and attitudes, especially their political ones, they will discover that the driving force is usually personal or national anger, hostility, and similar motives.

If this is the case, we must accept Islam and adopt an Islamic attitude as the fundamental starting point for action, rather than the existing oppressive situation. The Prophet defined true Muslims as those who harm no one with their words and actions, and who are the most trustworthy representatives of universal peace. Muslims travel everywhere with this sublime feeling that they nourish deep in their spirits. Contrary to inflicting torment and suffering, they are remembered as symbols of safety and security. In their eyes, there is no difference between a physical and a verbal violation, such as backbiting, false accusation, insult, and ridicule.

Our beginning point must have an Islamic basis. Muslims cannot act out of ideological or political partisanship and then dress it in Islamic garb or represent mere desires as ideas. If we can overcome this tendency, Islam's true image will become known. The present, distorted image of Islam that has resulted from its misuse, by both Muslims and non-Muslims for their own goals, scares both Muslims and non-Muslims.

Sidney Griffith points out one important fact of how the West views Islam: In American universities, Islam is not taught as a religion in theological schools but as a political system in the political science or international relations departments. Such a perception also is found among Westernized segments of the Islamic world and non-Muslims in Asia and Africa. Strangely enough, many groups that have put themselves forward under the banner of Islam export and actually strengthen this image.

Islam's Universal Call for Dialog

Fourteen centuries ago, Islam made the greatest ecumenical call the world has ever seen. The Qur'an calls the People of the Book[7]:

> Say: "O People of the Book! Come to common terms as between us and you: that we worship none but God; that we associate no partners with Him; that we take not, from among ourselves lords and patrons other than God." If then they turn back, say you: "Bear witness that we are Muslims (surrendered to God's Will)." (3:64)

This call, coming in the ninth year of the Hijra, begins with the *la* (no!) in the statement of faith *La ilaha illa Allah* (There is no deity but God). More than a command to do something positive, it is a call not to do certain things, so that followers of the revealed religions could overcome their mutual separation. It represented the widest statement on which members of all religions could agree. In case this call was rejected, Muslims were to respond: *Your religion is for you; my religion is for me* (109:6). That is, if you do not accept this call, we have surrendered to God. We will continue on the path we have accepted and let you go on your own path.

Elmalili Hamdi Yazir, a famous Turkish Qur'anic interpreter, made the following interesting observations regarding this verse:

> It has been shown how various consciences, nations, religions, and books can unite in one essential conscience and word of truth, and how Islam has taught the human realm such a wide, open, and true path of salvation and law of freedom. It has been shown fully that this is not limited to the Arab or non-Arab. Religious progress is possible not by consciences being narrow and separate from each other, but by their being universal and broad. [8]

Islam gave this breadth of conscience, this broad path of salvation, and this law of freedom to us as a gift. Bediüzzaman Said Nursi explains this broadest scope of Islam from a contemplative observation he had in the Bayezid Mosque in Istanbul:

> Once I thought about the pronoun "we" in the verse: *You alone do we worship, and You alone we ask for help* (1:5), and my heart sought the reason why "we" was used in place of "I." Suddenly I discovered the virtue and secret of congregational prayer from that pronoun "we."

> I saw that by doing my prayer with the congregation at the Bayezid Mosque, every individual in the congregation became a kind of intercessor for me, and as long as I recited the Qur'an there, everyone testified for me. I got the courage from the congregation's great and intense servitude to present my insufficient servitude to the Divine Court.

Suddenly another reality unveiled itself: All of Istanbul's mosques united and came under the authority of the Bayezid Mosque. I got the impression that they confirmed me in my cause and included me in their prayer. At that time I saw myself in the earthly mosque, in circular rows around the Ka'ba. I said: "Praise be to the Lord of the worlds. I have so many intercessors; they are saying the same thing I say in my prayer and confirming me."

As this reality was unveiled, I felt I was standing in prayer in front of the blessed Ka'ba. Taking advantage of this situation, I took those rows of worshipers as witnesses and said: "I witness that there is no deity but God; again I bear witness that Muhammad is God's Messenger." I entrusted this testimony to faith to the sacred Black Stone. While leaving this trust, suddenly another veil opened. I saw that the congregation I was in was separated into three circles.

The first circle was a large congregation of believing Muslims and those who believe in God's existence and Unity. In the second circle, I saw all creatures were performing the greatest prayer and invocation of God. Every class or species was busy with its own unique invocation and litanies to God, and I was among that congregation. In the third circle I saw an amazing realm that was outwardly small, but in reality, large from the perspective of the duty it performed and its quality. From the atoms of my body to the outer senses, there was a congregation busy with servitude and gratitude.

In short, the pronoun "we" in the expression "we worship" pointed to these three congregations. I imagined our Prophet, peace and blessings be upon him, the translator and propagator of the Qur'an, in Madina, from which he was addressing humanity, saying: *O humanity! Worship your Lord!* (2:21). Like everyone else, I heard his command in my spirit, and like me, everyone in the three congregations replied with the sentence: "You alone do we worship."'

How to Interact with Followers of Other Religions

In the Qur'an God says:

This is the Book; wherein there is no doubt; a guidance to the pious ones. (2:2)

Later it is explained that these pious ones are those:

Who believe in the Unseen, are steadfast in prayer, and spend out of what We have provided for them; and who believe in what is sent to you and what was sent before you, and (in their hearts) have the reassurance of the Hereafter (2:3-4).

At the very outset, using a very soft and slightly oblique style, the Qur'an calls people to accept the former Prophets and their Books. Having such a condition at the very beginning of the Qur'an seems very important to me when it comes to starting a dialog with the followers of other religions. In another verse God commands:

And discuss you not with the People of the Book, except with means better (than mere disputation). (29:46)

This verse describes what method, approach, and manner should be used. Bediüzzaman's view of the form and style of debate are extremely significant: "Anyone who is happy about defeating an opponent in debate is without mercy." He explains further: "You gain nothing by such a defeat. If you were defeated and the other was victorious, you would have corrected one of your mistakes." Debate should not be for the sake of our ego, but to enable the truth to come out. Elsewhere it is stated:

> God forbids you not, with regard to those who fight you not for (your) Faith nor drive you out of your homes, from dealing kindly and justly with them: for God loves those who are just. (60:8)

According to some, several verses harshly criticize the People of the Book. In reality, such criticism is directed against wrong behavior, incorrect thought, resistance to truth, the creation of hostility, and undesirable characteristics. The Bible contains even stronger criticisms of the same attributes. However, immediately after these apparently sharp criticisms and threats, very gentle words are used to awaken hearts to the truth and to plant hope. In addition, the Qur'an's criticism and warning about some attitudes and behavior found among Jews, Christians, and polytheists also were directed toward Muslims who still indulged in them. Both the Companions and expounders of the Qur'an agree on this.

God-revealed religions strongly oppose disorder, treachery, conflict, and oppression. Islam literally means "peace," "security," and "well-being." Naturally based on peace, security, and world harmony, it sees war and conflict as aberrations to be brought under control. An exception is made for self-defense, as when a body tries to defeat the germs attacking it. Self-defense must follow certain guidelines, however. Islam always has breathed peace and goodness. Considering war an accident, it established rules to balance and limit it. For example, it takes justice and world peace as a basis, as in:

> Let not the hatred of others to you make you swerve to wrong and depart from justice. (5:8)

Islam developed a line of defense based on principles that protect religion, life, property, the mind, and reproduction. The modern legal system also has done this.

Islam accords the greatest value to human life. It views the killing of one person as the killing of all people, for a single murder engenders the idea that any person can be killed. Adam's son Cain was the first murderer. Although their names are not specifically mentioned in the Qur'an or Sunna, we learn from the Bible that a misunderstanding between Cain and Abel resulted in Cain unjustly killing Abel in a jealous rage. And thus began the epoch of spilling blood. For this reason, one hadith records the Messenger of God as saying: "Whenever a person is killed unjustly, part of the sin for murder is credited to Adam's son Cain, for he opened to humanity the way of unjust killing." The Qur'an also states that one who kills a person unjustly in effect has killed everyone, and one who saves another in effect has saved everyone (5:32).

Love, Compassion, Tolerance, and Forgiving: The Pillars of Dialog

Religion commands love, compassion, tolerance, and

forgiving. Therefore, I would like to say a few words concerning these fundamental universal values.

Love is the most essential element in every being, a most radiant light, a great power that can resist and overcome every force. It elevates every soul that absorbs it, and prepares it for the journey to eternity. Those who make contact with eternity through love work to implant in all other souls what they receive from eternity. They dedicate their lives to this sacred duty, and endure any hardship for its sake. Just as they say "love" with their last breaths, they also breathe "love" while being raised on the Day of Judgment.

Altruism, an exalted human feeling, generates love. Whoever has the greatest share in this love is humanity's greatest hero, one who has uprooted any personal feelings of hatred and rancor. Such heroes continue to live even after death. These lofty souls, who daily light a new torch of love in their inner world and make their hearts a source of love and altruism, are welcomed and loved by people. They receive the right of eternal life from such an Exalted Court. Not even death or Doomsday can remove their traces.

Love, the most direct way to someone's heart, is the Prophets' way. Those who follow it are not rejected. Even if some reject them, far more others welcome them. Once they are welcomed through love, nothing prevents them from attaining their goal.

Everything speaks of and promises compassion. Therefore, the universe can be considered as a symphony of compassion. A human being must show compassion to all living beings, for this is a requirement of being human. The more people display compassion, the more exalted they become; the more they resort to wrongdoing, oppression, and cruelty, the more they are disgraced and humiliated. They become a shame to humanity. We hear from Prophet Muhammad that a prostitute went to Paradise because out of compassion she gave water to a dog dying of thirst, while another woman went to Hell because she allowed a cat to starve to death.

Forgiving is a great virtue. Forgiveness cannot be considered as separate from virtue, or virtue as separate from forgiveness. Everyone knows the adage: "Mistakes from the small, forgiveness from the great." How true this is! Being forgiven means a repair, a return to an essence, and finding oneself again. For this reason, the most pleasing action in the Infinite Mercy's view is activity pursued amidst the palpitations of this return and search.

All of creation, both animate and inanimate, was introduced to forgiveness through humanity. Just as God showed His Attribute of Forgiveness through individual human beings, He put the beauty of forgiving in their hearts. While Adam, the first man, dealt a blow to his essence through falling, which is somehow a requirement of his human nature, God's forgiveness gave him a hand and elevated him to the rank of Prophethood.

Whenever people have erred, mounting on the magic transport of seeking forgiveness and surmounting the shame of personal sin and the resulting despair, they attain infinite mercy and overlook the sins of others. Jesus said to a crowd of people eager to stone a woman: "If anyone of you is without sin let him be the first to throw a stone at her."[10] Can anyone who understands this binding, fine point even consider stoning someone else when he or she is also a likely candidate for being stoned? If only those unfortunate ones who demand that others pass a certain litmus test could understand this!

Malice and hatred are the seeds of hell scattered among people by evil. In contrast to those who encourage such evil and turn the land into a pit of Hell, we should carry forgiveness to those whose troubles are pushing them into the abyss. The excesses of those who neither forgive nor tolerate others have made the past one or two centuries the most horrific of all time. If such people are to rule the future, it will be a fearful time indeed. Thus the greatest gift today's generation can give to its children and grandchildren is to teach them how to forgive, even in the face of the crudest behavior and most upsetting events. We believe that forgiveness and tolerance will heal most of our wounds only if this celestial instrument is in the hands of those who understand its language.

Our tolerance should be so broad that we can close our eyes to others' faults, show respect for different ideas, and forgive everything that is forgivable. Even when our inalienable rights are violated, we should respect human values and try to establish justice. Even before the coarsest thoughts and crudest ideas, with a Prophet's caution and without boiling over, we should respond with a mildness that the Qur'an calls "gentle words." We should do this so that we can touch other people's hearts by following a method consisting of a tender heart, a gentle approach, and mild behavior. We should have such a broad tolerance that we benefit from contradictory ideas, for they force us to keep our heart, spirit, and conscience in good shape even though they teach us nothing.

Tolerance, which we sometimes use in place of respect and mercy, generosity and forbearance, is the most essential element of moral systems. It also is a very important source of spiritual discipline, and a celestial virtue of perfected men and women.

Under the lens of tolerance, the believers' merits attain a new depth and extend to infinity; mistakes and faults shrink into insignificance. Actually, the treatment of He Who is beyond time and space always passes through the prism of tolerance, and we wait for it to embrace us and all of creation. This embrace is so broad that a prostitute who gave water to a thirsty dog touched the knocker of the "Door of Mercy" and found herself in a corridor extending to Heaven. Due to the deep love he felt for God and His Messenger, an alcoholic suddenly shook himself free and became a Companion of the Prophet. And, with the smallest of Divine favors, a murderer was saved from his monstrous psychosis, turned toward the highest rank, which far surpassed his natural ability, and reached it.

We want everyone to look at us through this lens, and we expect the breezes of forgiveness and pardon to blow constantly in our surroundings. All of us want to refer our past and present to the climate of tolerance and forbearance, which melts and transforms, cleans and purifies, and then walk toward the future without anxiety. We do not want our past to be criticized, or our future to be darkened because of our present. All of us expect love and respect, hope for tolerance and forgiveness, and want to be embraced with feelings of liberality and affection. We expect tolerance and forgiveness from our parents in response to our mischief at home, from our teachers in response to our naughtiness at school, from the innocent victims of our injustice and oppression, from the judge and prosecutor in court, and from the Judge of Judges (God) in the highest tribunal.

However, deserving what we expect is very important. One who does not forgive cannot expect forgiveness. We will see disrespect to the extent we have been disrespectful. One who does not love is not worthy of being loved. One who does not embrace humanity with tolerance and forgiveness will not receive forgiveness and pardon. One who curses others can expect only curses in return. Those who curse will be cursed, and those who beat will be beaten. If true Muslims would continue on their way and tolerate curses with such Qur'anic principles as: *When they meet empty words or unseemly behavior, they generously pass them by and if you behave tolerantly and overlook their faults*, others would appear to implement the justice of Destiny on those cursers.

The Last Word

Those who want to reform the world must first reform themselves. In order to bring others to the path of traveling to a better world, they must purify their inner worlds of hatred, rancor, and jealousy, and adorn their outer worlds with virtue. Those who are far removed from self-control and self-discipline, who have failed to refine their feelings, may seem attractive and insightful at first. However, they will not be able to inspire others in any permanent way, and the sentiments they arouse will soon disappear.

Goodness, beauty, truthfulness, and being virtuous are the essence of the world and humanity. Whatever happens, the world will one day find this essence. No one can prevent this.

Endnotes:

This article was presented originally as a paper at the Parliament of the World's Religions, Cape Town, Dec. 1-8, 1999. It appeared as a revised edition in *Turkish Daily News* (January 11-12, 2000) and *The Fountain* 3:31 (July-Sept. 2000): 7-8.

1   Ismail, R. Faruqi, *İbrahimi Dinlerin Diyaloğu*, (trans.), Istanbul, 1995, 51-53. Originally published as *Dialog of the Abrahamic Faiths*.

2   Graham E. Fuller and Ian O. Lesser, *Kuşatılanlar-İslam ve Batı'nın Jeopolitiği*, (trans.), Istanbul, 1996, 41-42. Originally published as *A Sense of Siege: The Geopolitics of Islam and the West.*

3   Sidney Griffith, "Sharing the Faith of Abraham: The 'Credo' of Louis Massignon," *Islam and Christian-Muslim Relations* 8, no. 2:193-210.

4   Translated from Suat Yıldırım, *"Kiliseyi İslam ile Diyalog İstemeye Sevkeden Sebepler"* (What Drived the Church to Dialog with Islam?) (trans.), Yeni Ümit, no 16, 7.

5   Abu'l-Fazl Ezzati, *İslam'ın Yayılış Tarihine Giriş* (trans.), İstanbul, 1984, 348.

6   Sidney Griffith, *Zaman.*

7   Although *ahl al-kitab*, "People of the Book," is commonly considered to be referring to Christians and Jews, Islamic tradition accepts, in general terms, other belief systems like Zoroastrians, Buddhists, or Hindus under the same category, as their major tenets of faith are similar to that of Islam's.

8   Elmalılı Hamdi Yazır, *Hak Dini Kur'an Dili*, Istanbul, 2:1131-32.

9   Said Nursi, *The Letters*, 29th Letter.

10   Gospel of John, Chapter 8, Verse 7.

Islam as a Religion of Universal Mercy

L ife is God's foremost and most manifest blessing, and the true and everlasting life is that of the Hereafter. Since we can deserve this life by pleasing God, He sent Prophets and revealed Scriptures out of His compassion for us. For this reason, while mentioning His blessings upon humanity in *Sura al-Rahman* (the All-Merciful), He begins: *Al-Rahman. He taught the Qur'an, created humanity, and taught it speech* (55:1-4).

All aspects of this life are a rehearsal for the afterlife, and every creature is engaged toward this end. Order is evident in every effort, and compassion resides in every achievement. Some "natural" events or social convulsions may seem disagreeable at first, but we should not regard them as incompatible with compassion. They are like dark clouds or lightning and thunder that, although frightening, nevertheless bring us good tidings of rain. Thus the whole universe praises the All-Compassionate.

Prophet Muhammad is like a spring of pure water in the heart of a desert, a source of light in an all-enveloping darkness. Mercy was like a magical key in the Prophet's hands, for with it he opened hearts that were so hardened and rusty that no one thought they could be opened. But he did even more: he lit a torch of belief in them.

God's Messenger preached Islam, the religion of universal mercy. However, some self-proclaimed humanists say it is "a religion of the sword." This is completely wrong.

Similarly, it is quite important to apportion compassion and identify who deserves it, for "compassion for a wolf sharpens its appetite, and not being content with what it receives, it demands even more." Compassion for wrongdoers makes them more aggressive and encourages them to work against others. In fact, true compassion requires that such people be prevented from doing wrong. When God's Messenger told his Companions to help people when they were just and unjust, they asked him to explain this seeming paradox. He replied: "You help such people by preventing them from engaging in injustice." So, compassion requires that those who cause trouble either be deprived of their means for doing so or be stopped. Otherwise, they eventually will take control and do as they please.

The compassion of God's Messenger encompassed every creature. He knew that allowing blood-stained, blood-thirsty people to control others would be the most terrible form of tyranny imaginable. Therefore, out of compassion, he required that lambs should be able to live in security against the wolves' attacks. He desired, of course, that everyone be guided. In fact, this was his greatest concern: *Yet it may be, if they believe not in this Message, you will consume yourself, following after them, with grief* (18:6). When he was wounded severely at Uhud, he raised his hands and prayed: "O God, forgive my people, for they don't know."

The Makkans, his own people, inflicted so much suffering on him that he finally emigrated to Madina. Even after that, the next 5 years were far from being peaceful. However, when he conquered Makka without bloodshed in the twenty-first year of his Prophethood, he asked the Makkan unbelievers: "How do you expect me to treat you?" They responded unanimously: "You are a noble one, the son of a noble one." He then told them his decision: "You may leave, for no reproach this day shall be on you. May God forgive you. He is the Most Compassionate."[1]

The Messenger displayed the highest degree of compassion toward believers: *There has come to you a Messenger from among yourselves; grievous to him is your suffering; anxious is he over you, full of concern for you, for the believers full of pity, compassionate* (9:128). *He lowered unto believers his wing of tenderness through mercy* (15:88), and was the *guardian of believers and nearer to them than their selves* (33:6).

His compassion even encompassed the Hypocrites and unbelievers. He knew who the Hypocrites were, but never identified them, for this would have deprived them of the rights of full citizenship they had gained by their outward confession of faith and practice.

As for unbelievers, God removed their collective destruction, although He had eradicated many such people in the past: *But God would never chastise them while you*

*were among them; God would never chastise them as
they begged forgiveness* (8:33). This verse refers to unbelievers of whatever time. God will not destroy peoples
altogether as long as those who follow the Messenger are
alive. Besides, He has left the door of repentance open un-
til the Last Day. Anyone can accept Islam or ask God's forgiveness, regardless of how sinful they consider themselves to be.

For this reason, a Muslim's enmity toward unbelievers
is a form of pity. When 'Umar saw an 80-year-old unbe-
lieving one, he sat down and sobbed. When asked why he
did so, he replied: "God assigned him so long a life span,
but he has not been able to find the true path." 'Umar
was a disciple of God's Messenger, who said: "I was not
sent to call down curses on people, but as a mercy"[2] and
"I am Muhammad, and Ahmad (praised one), and Mu-
qaffi (the Last Prophet); I am Hashir (the final Prophet
in whose presence the dead will be resurrected); the
Prophet of repentance (the Prophet for whom the door
of repentance will always remain open), and the Prophet
of mercy."[3]

God's Messenger was particularly compassionate toward children. When he saw a child crying, he sat beside
him or her and shared his or her feelings. He felt the pain
of a mother for her child more than the mother herself.
Once he said: "I stand in prayer and wish to prolong it.
However, I hear a child cry and shorten the prayer to less-
en the mother's anxiety."[4]

He took children in his arms and hugged them. Once
when hugging his beloved grandsons, Hasan and Hus-

ayn, Aqra ibn Habis told him: "I have 10 children, none of whom I have ever kissed." God's Messenger responded: "One without pity for others is not pitied."[5] According to another version, he added: "What can I do for you if God has removed compassion from you?"[6]

Once he said: "Pity those on Earth so that those in the Heavens will pity you."[7] Once when Sa'd ibn 'Ubada became ill, God's Messenger visited him at home and, seeing his faithful Companion in a pitiful state, began to cry. He said: "God does not punish because of tears or grief, but He punishes because of this," and he pointed to his tongue.[8] When 'Uthman ibn Mad'un died, he wept profusely.

A member of the Banu Muqarrin clan once beat his maidservant. She informed God's Messenger, who sent for the master. He said: "You have beaten her without any justifiable right. Free her."[9] Freeing a slave free was far better for the master than being punished in the Hereafter because of that act. God's Messenger always protected and supported widows, orphans, the poor and disabled even before announcing his Prophethood. When he returned home in excitement from Mount Hira after the first Revelation, his wife Khadija told him: "I hope you will be the Prophet of this Umma, for you always tell the truth, fulfill your trust, support your relatives, help the poor and weak, and feed guests."[10]

His compassion even encompassed animals. We hear from him: "A prostitute was guided to truth by God and ultimately went to Paradise because she gave water to a poor dog dying of thirst. Another woman was sent to

Hell because she let a cat die of hunger."[11] Once while returning from a military campaign, a few Companions removed some young birds from their nest to stroke them. The mother bird came back and, not finding its babies, began to fly around screeching. When told of this, God's Messenger became angry and ordered the birds to be put back in the nest.[12]

While in Mina, some of his Companions attacked a snake in order to kill it. However, it managed to escape. Watching this from afar, God's Messenger remarked: "It was saved from your evil, as you were from its evil."[13] Ibn 'Abbas reported that God's Messenger once saw a man sharpening his knife directly before the sheep to be slaughtered, and asked him: "Do you want to kill it many times?"[14]

He eradicated all differences of race and color. Once Abu Dharr got so angry with Bilal that he insulted him: "You son of a black woman!" Bilal came to God's Messenger and reported the incident in tears. The Messenger reproached Abu Dharr: "Do you still have a sign of Jahiliyya?" Full of repentance, Abu Dharr lay on the ground and said: "I won't raise my head (meaning he wouldn't get up) unless Bilal put his foot on it to pass over it." Bilal forgave him, and they were reconciled.[15]

Endnotes:

This article originally appeared in Fethullah Gulen, *Sonsuz Nur*, 9th ed. (Izmir: Nil Yayinlari, 1997), 1:377-97.
1   Ibn Hisham, Sira al-Nabawiya, 4:55; Ibn Kathir, *al-Bidaya wa al-Nihaya*, 4:344.
2   Muslim, *Sahih*, "Birr," 87.
3   Ahmad ibn Hanbal, *Musnad*, 4:395; Muslim, *Sahih*, "Fada'il," 126.
4   Bukhari, *Sahih*, "Adhan," 65; Muslim, *Sahih*, "Salat," 192.

5   Sahih al-Bukhari, "Adab," 18.

6   Bukhari, *Sahih*, "Adab," 18; Muslim, *Sahih*, "Fada'il," 64; Ibn Maja, *Sunan*, "Adab," 3.

7   Tirmidhi, *Sunan*, "Birr," 16.

8   Bukhari, Sahih "Jana'iz," 45; Muslim, Sahih, "Jana'iz," 12.

9   Muslim, *Sahih*, "Ayman," 31, 33; Ibn Hanbal, *Musnad*, 3:447.

10 Ibn Sa'd, *al-Tabaqat al-Kubra'*, 1:195.

11 Bukhari, *Sahih*, "Anbiya'," 54, "Musaqat," 9; Muslim, *Sahih*, "Salam," 153; Ibn Hanbal, *Musnad*, 2:507.

12 Abu Dawud, *Sunan*, "Adab," 164, "Jihad," 112; Ibn Hanbal, *Musnad*, 1:404.

13 Nasa'i, *Sunan*, "Hajj," 114; I, Hanbal, *Musnad*, 1:385.

14 Hakim, *Mustadrak*, 4:231, 233.

15 Bukhari, *Sahih*, "Iman," 22.

Jihad with Its Lesser and Greater Kinds or Aspects

(Jihad is one of the subjects most misunderstood by both Westerners and Muslims. Fethullah Gülen analyzes this topic in his book *I'la-yi Kelimetullah veya Cihad* (Glorifying God's Name: Jihad) and in the answer he gave to a specific question. The following are highlights of his views explained in his book and answer.)

What Is Jihad?

Derived from the root *j-h-d*, jihad means using all one's strength, as well as moving toward an objective with all one's power and strength and resisting every difficulty.

Jihad gained a special characteristic with the advent of Islam: striving in the path of God. This is the meaning that usually comes to mind today. This striving occurs on two fronts: the internal and the external. The internal one can be described as the effort to attain one's essence; the external one as the process of enabling someone else to attain his or her essence. The first is the greater jihad; the second is the lesser jihad. The first is based on overcoming obstacles between oneself and his or her essence, and the soul's reaching knowledge and eventually divine knowledge, divine love, and spiritual bliss. The second is based on removing obstacles between people and faith so that people can have a free choice to adopt a way.

Kinds of Jihad

The lesser jihad does not mean to fight on the battlefronts exclusively. In reality, the lesser jihad has so broad a meaning and application that sometimes a word or silence, a frown or a smile, leaving or entering an assembly—in short, everything done for God's sake—and regulating love and anger according to His approval is included in it. In this way, all efforts made to reform society and people are part of jihad, as is every effort made for your family, relatives, neighbors, and region.

In a sense, the lesser jihad is material. The greater jihad, however, is conducted on the spiritual front, for it is our struggle with our inner world and ego (*nafs*). When both of these are carried out successfully, the desired balance is established. If one is missing, the balance is destroyed. Believers find peace and vitality in such a balanced jihad.

There are as many roads to God as there are creatures. God leads those who strive for His sake to salvation on one or more of these roads. He opens each road to goodness and protects it from the roads to evil. Everyone who finds His road finds the middle road. Just as these people follow a middle path regarding anger, intelligence, and lust, so do they follow a middle way regarding jihad and worship. This means that God has led humanity to the path of salvation.

The lesser jihad is our active fulfillment of God's commands; the greater jihad is proclaiming war on our ego's destructive and negative emotions and thoughts (e.g., malice, hatred, envy, selfishness, pride, arrogance, and pomp), which prevent us from attaining perfection. As this is a very difficult and hard jihad, it is called the great-er jihad. Those who fail in the greater jihad will fail in the lesser jihad.

'A'isha related:

> One night the Messenger of God asked: "'A'isha, can I spend this night with my Lord?" (He was refined enough to seek such permission. Nobility and refinement were im-portant aspects of his profundity.) I replied: "Messenger of God, I would like to be with you, but I'd like what you like even more." The Prophet made ablution and began pray-ing. He recited: *Behold! In the creation of the heavens and earth, and the alternation of night and day—there are in-deed Signs for people of understanding* (3:190). He recit-ed this verse and shed tears until morning.[1]

This shows the inner depth and greater jihad of our Prophet.

Jihad is a balance of internal and external conquest. Reaching spiritual perfection and helping others do so are points of consideration. Attaining internal perfection is the greater jihad; helping others attain it is the lesser jihad. When you separate one from the other, jihad is no longer jihad. Indolence is born from one and anarchy from the other. How happy are those who search for a way to salvation for others as much as they do for them-selves. And how happy are those who remember to save themselves while saving others!

Endnotes:

This article originally appeared in Fethullah Gülen, *I'la-yi Kelimetullah veya Cihad* (Izmir: Nil Yayinlari, 1998) and *Asrin Getirdigi Tereddütler* (Izmir: T.Ö.V. Yayine-vi, 1997) 3:186-219.

1   Ibn Kathir, *Tafsir (Âl 'Imran)*, 190.Interview with M. Fethullah Gülen

M. Fethullah Gülen
and Education

Fethullah Gülen is an educationist. He is an educator of not only mind but also heart and spirit. He is reputed especially for his endeavoring people to establish educational institutions both in Turkey and abroad. In this section you will find his views of education and the educational activities of Turkish entrepreneurs outside Turkey.

Education from Cradle to Grave

Introduction

The main duty and purpose of human life is to seek understanding. The effort of doing so, known as education, is a perfecting process though which we earn, in the spiritual, intellectual, and physical dimensions of their beings, the rank appointed for us as the perfect pattern of creation. At birth, the outset of the earthly phase of our journey from the world of spirits to eternity, we are wholly impotent and needy. By contrast, most animals come into the world as if matured or perfected beforehand. Within a few hours or days or months, they learn everything necessary for their survival, as well as how to relate to their environment and with other creatures. For example, sparrows or bees acquire maturity and all the physical and social skills they need within about 20 days; we need 20 years or more to acquire a comparable level of maturity.

We are born helpless as well as ignorant of the laws of life and must cry out to get the help we need. After a year or so, we can stand on our feet and walk a little. When we are about 15, we are expected to have understood the difference between good and evil, the beneficial and the harmful. However, it will take us our whole lives to acquire intellectual and spiritual perfection. Our principal duty in life is to acquire perfection and purity in our thinking, conceptions, and belief. By fulfilling our duty of servanthood to the Creator, Nourisher, and Protector, and by penetrating the mystery of creation through our potentials and faculties, we seek to attain to the rank of true humanity and become worthy of a blissful, eternal life in another, exalted world.

Our humanity is directly proportional to our emotions' purity. Although those who are full of bad feelings and whose souls are influenced by egoism look like human beings, whether they really are human is doubtful. Almost everyone can train their bodies, but few can educate their minds and feelings. The former training produces strong bodies, while the latter produces spiritual people.

Our Innate Faculties and Education

Since the time of Ibn Miskawayh, human faculties or "drives" have been dealt with in three categories: reason, anger, and lust.[1] Reason encompasses all of our powers of conception, imagination, calculation, memory, learning, and so on. Anger covers our power of self-defense, which Islamic jurisprudence defines as that needed to defend our faith and religion, sanity, possessions, life and family, and other sacred values. Lust is the name for the driving force of our animal appetites:

> Decked out for humanity is the passionate love of desires for the opposite sex and offspring; for hoarded treasures of

gold and silver; for branded horses, cattle, and plantations; and for all kinds of worldly things. (3:14)

These drives are found in other creatures. However, whether in their desires, intelligence, or determination to defend life and territory, these drives are limited in all creatures but humanity. Each of us is uniquely endowed with free will and the consequent obligation to discipline our powers. This struggle for discipline determines our humanity. In combination with each other and with circumstances, our faculties often are expressed through jealousy, hatred, enmity, hypocrisy, and show. They also need to be disciplined.

We are not only composed of body and mind. Each of us has a spirit that needs satisfaction. Without this, we cannot find true happiness and perfection. Spiritual satisfaction is possible only through knowledge of God and belief in Him. Confined within the physical world, our own particular carnal self, time, and place can be experienced as a dungeon. We can escape it through belief and regular worship, and by refraining from extremes while using our faculties or powers. We must not seek to annul our drives, but to use our free will to contain and purify them, to channel and direct them toward virtue. For example, we are not expected to eliminate lust, but to satisfy it lawfully through reproduction. Happiness lies in confining our lust to the lawful bounds of decency and chastity, not in engaging in debauchery and dissipation.

Similarly, jealousy can be channeled into emulation free of rancor, which inspires us to emulate those who excel in goodness and good deeds. Applying the proper discipline to our reason results in the acquisition of knowledge, and ultimately of understanding or wisdom. Purifying and training anger leads to courage and forbearance. Disciplining our passion and desire develops our chastity.

If every virtue is thought of as the center of a circle, and any movement away from the center as a vice, the vice becomes greater as we move further away from the center. Every virtue therefore has innumerable vices, since there is only one center in a circle but an infinite number of points around it. It is irrelevant in which direction the deviation occurs, for deviation from the center, in whatever direction, is a vice.

There are two extremes related to each moral virtue: deficiency or excess. The two extremes connected with wisdom are stupidity and cunning. For courage they are cowardice and rashness, and for chastity they are lethargy and uncontrolled lust. So a person's perfection, the ultimate purpose of our existence, lies in maintaining a condition of balance and moderation between the two extremes relating to every virtue. 'Ali ibn Abi Talib is reported to have said:

> God has characterized angels by intellect without sexual desire, passion, and anger, and animals with anger and desire without intellect. He exalted humanity by bestowing upon them all of these qualities. Accordingly, if a person's intellect dominates his or her desire and ferocity, he or she rises to a station above that of angels, because this station is attained by a human being in spite of the existence of obstacles that do not vex angels.

Improving a community is possible only by elevating the

young generations to the rank of humanity, not by obliterating the bad ones. Unless a seed composed of religion, tradition, and historical consciousness is germinated throughout the country, new evil elements will appear and grow in the place of each eradicated bad one.

The Real Meaning and Value of Education

Education through learning and a commendable way of life is a sublime duty that manifests the Divine Name *Rabb* (Upbringer and Sustainer). By fulfilling it, we attain the rank of true humanity and become a beneficial element of society.

Education is vital for both societies and individuals. First, our humanity is directly proportional to our emotions' purity. Although those who are full of bad feelings and whose souls are influenced by egoism look like human beings, whether they really are so is questionable. Almost anyone can be successful in physical training, but few can educate their minds and feelings. Second, improving a community is possible by elevating the coming generations to the rank of humanity, not by obliterating the bad ones. Unless the seeds of religion, traditional values, and historical consciousness germinate throughout the country, new bad elements will inevitably grow up in the place of every bad element that has been eradicated.

A nation's future depends on its youth. Any people who want to secure their future should apply as much energy to raising their children as they devote to other issues. A nation that fails its youth, that abandons them to foreign cultural influences, jeopardizes their identity and is subject to cultural and political weakness.

The reasons for the vices observed in today's generation, as well as the incompetence of some administrators and other nation-wide troubles, lie in the prevailing conditions and ruling elite of 25 years ago. Likewise, those who are charged with educating today's young people will be responsible for the vices and virtues that will appear in another 25 years. Those who wish to predict a nation's future can do so correctly by taking a full account of the education and upbringing given to its young people. "Real" life is possible only through knowledge. Thus, those who neglect learning and teaching should be counted as "dead" even though they are living, for we were created to learn and communicate to others what we have learned.

Right decisions depend on having a sound mind and being capable of sound thought. Science and knowledge illuminate and develop the mind. For this reason, a mind deprived of science and knowledge cannot reach right decisions, is always exposed to deception, and is subject to being misled.

We are only truly human if we learn, teach, and inspire others. It is difficult to regard those who are ignorant and without desire to learn as truly human. It is also questionable whether learned people who do not renew and reform themselves in order to set an example for others are truly human. Status and merit acquired through knowledge and science are higher and more lasting than those obtained through other means.

Given the great importance of learning and teaching, we must determine what is to be learned and taught, and when and how to do so. Although knowledge is a value in itself, the purpose of learning is to make knowledge a guide in life and illuminate the road to human betterment. Thus, any knowledge not appropriated for the self is a burden to the learner, and a science that does not direct one toward sublime goals is a deception.

But knowledge acquired for a right purpose is an inexhaustible source of blessings for the learner. Those who possess such a source are always sought by people, like a source of fresh water, and lead people to the good. Knowledge limited to empty theories and unabsorbed pieces of learning, which arouses suspicions in minds and darkens hearts, is a "heap of garbage" around which desperate and confused souls flounder. Therefore, science and knowledge should seek to uncover humanity's nature and creation's mysteries. Any knowledge, even "scientific," is true only if it sheds light on the mysteries of human nature and the dark areas of existence.

- The future of every individual is closely related to the impressions and influences experienced during childhood and youth. If children and young people are brought up in a climate where their enthusiasm is stimulated with higher feelings, they will have vigorous minds and display good morals and virtues.

- Although it is fundamental that girls be brought up to be delicate like flowers and mild and affectionate educators of children, due attention must be given to making them inflexible defenders of truth. Otherwise, we shall have transformed them into poor, impotent beings for the sake of delicacy and mildness. We must not forget that female lions are still lions.

Family, School, and Environment

People who want to guarantee their future cannot be indifferent how their children are being educated. The family, school, environment, and mass media should cooperate to ensure the desired result. Opposing tendencies among these vital institutions will subject young people to contradictory influences that will distract them and dissipate their energy. In particular, the mass media should contribute to young people's education by following the education policy approved by the community. The school must be as perfect as possible with respect to curriculum, its teachers' scientific and moral standards of teachers, and its physical conditions. A family must provide the necessary warmth and quality of atmosphere in which the children are raised.

In the early centuries of Islam, minds, hearts, and souls strove to understand that which the Lord of the heavens and the Earth approves. Each conversation, discussion, correspondence, and event was directed to that end. As a result, whoever could do so imbibed the right values and spirit from the surrounding environment. It was as if everything was a teacher to prepare the individual's mind and soul and develop his or her capacity to attain a high level in Islamic sciences. The first school in which we receive the necessary education to be perfected is the home.

The home is vital to raising of a healthy generation and ensuring a healthy social system or structure. This responsibility continues throughout life. The impressions we receive from our family cannot be deleted later in life. Furthermore, the family's control over the child at home, with respect to other siblings and toys, continues at school, with respect to the child's friends, books, and places visited. Parents must feed their children's minds with knowledge and science before their minds become engaged in useless things, for souls without truth and knowledge are fields in which evil thoughts are cultivated and grown.

Children can receive a good education at home only if there is a healthy family life. Thus marriage should be undertaken to form a healthy family life and so contribute to the permanence of one's nation in particular, and of the human population in general. Peace, happiness, and security at home is the mutual accord between the spouses in thought, morals, and belief. Couples who decide to marry should know each other very well and consider purity of feelings, chastity, morality, and virtue rather than wealth and physical charm. Children's mischief and impudence reflect the atmosphere in which they are being raised. A dysfunctional family life increasingly reflects upon the child's spirit, and therefore upon society.

In the family, elders should treat those younger than them with compassion, and the young should show respect for their elders. Parents should love and respect each other, and treat their children with compassion and due consideration of their feelings. They must treat each child justly and not discriminate among them. If parents encourage their children to develop their abilities and be useful to themselves and the community, they have given the nation a strong new pillar. If they do not cultivate the proper feelings in their children, they release scorpions into the community.

- Good manners are a virtue and are greatly appreciated in whomever they are found. Those with good manners are liked, even if they are uneducated. Communities devoid of culture and education are like rude individuals, for one cannot find in them any loyalty in friendship or consistency in enmity. Those who trust such people are always disappointed, and those who depend upon them are left, sooner or later, without support.

The School and the Teacher

A school may be considered a laboratory that offers an elixir that can prevent or heal the ills of life. Those who have the knowledge and wisdom to prepare and administer it are the teachers.

A school is a place of learning about everything related to this life and the next. It can shed light on vital ideas and events, and enable its students to understand their natural and human environment. It also can quickly open the way to unveiling the meaning of things and events, thereby leading a student to wholeness of thought and contemplation. In essence, a school is a kind of place of worship whose "holy people" are teachers.

Real teachers sow the pure seed and preserve it. They occupy themselves with what is good and wholesome, and lead and guide the children in life and whatever events they encounter. For a school to be a true institution of education, students first should be equipped with an ideal, a love of their language and how to use it most effectively, good morals, and perennial human values. Their social identity must be built on these foundations.

Education is different from teaching. Most people can teach, but only a very few can educate. Communities composed of individuals devoid of a sublime ideal, good manners, and human values are like rude individuals who have no loyalty in friendship or consistency in enmity. Those who trust such people are always disappointed, and those who depend upon them are sooner or later left without support. The best way of equipping one with such values is a sound religious education.

A community's survival depends on idealism and good morals, as well as on reaching the necessary level in scientific and technological progress. For this reason, trades and crafts should be taught beginning at least in the elementary level. A good school is not a building where only theoretical information is given, but an institution or a laboratory where students are prepared for life.

Patience is of great importance in education. Educating people is the most sacred, but also the most difficult, task in life. In addition to setting a good personal example, teachers should be patient enough to obtain the desired result. They should know their students very well, and address their intellects and their hearts, spirits, and feelings. The best way to educate people is to show a special concern for every individual, not forgetting that each individual is a different "world."

School provides its pupils with the possibilities of continuous reading, and speaks even when it is silent. Because of this, although it seems to occupy only one phase of life, school actually dominates all times and events. For the rest of their lives, pupils re-enact what they learned at school and derive continuous influence therefrom. Teachers should know how to find a way to the student's heart and leave indelible imprints upon his or her mind. They should test the information to be passed on to students by refining their own minds and the prisms of their hearts. A good lesson is one that does more than provide pupils with useful information or skills; it should elevate them into the presence of the unknown. This enables the students to acquire a penetrating vision into the reality of things, and to see each event as a sign of the unseen world.[2]

Educational Services Spreading throughout the World

Many things have been said and written about education. We will approach this subject from three interrelated angles: human–psychological, national–social, and universal.

We have been under the serious influence of contemporary Western thought, which undoubtedly has many superior aspects, for several centuries. However, it also has some defects stemming especially from the historical period it passed through and the unique conditions it created. In the Middle Ages, when Europe was living under a theocratic order ruled by the Church or Church-appointed monarchs, it came into contact with the Islamic world, especially through Andalusia and the Crusades. In addition to other factors, this opened the door for the Renaissance and Reform movements. Together with such other factors as land shortages, poverty, the drive to meet growing needs, and some island nations like England being naturally inclined to sea transportation, it also led to overseas geographical discoveries.

The primary drive in all of these developments was to satisfy material needs. As the accompanying scientific studies developed in opposition to the Church and medieval Chris-tian scholasticism, Europeans were confronted with a religion–science conflict.[3] This caused religion to split off from science and many people to break with religion. This development eventually led to materialism and communism. In social geography, humanity was faced with the most striking elements of Western history: global exploitation, unending conflict based on interest, two world wars, and the division of the world into blocs.

The West has held the world under its economic and military control for several centuries. In recent centuries, its religion–science conflict has occupied many intellectual circles. Enlightenment movements beginning in the eighteenth century saw human beings as mind only. Following that, positivist and materialist movements saw them as material or corporeal entities only. As a result, spiritual crises have followed one after another. It is no exaggeration to say that these crises and the absence of spiritual satisfaction were the major factors behind the conflict of interests that enveloped the last two centuries and reached its apex in the two world wars.

As possessors of a system of belief with a different history and essence, we have some basic things to give to the West, with whom we have deep economic, social, and even military relationships, and to humanity at large. At the head of these are our understanding and view of humanity. This view is neither exclusive to us or subjective; rather, it is an objective view that puts forward what we really are.

We are creatures composed of not only a body or mind or feelings or spirit; rather, we are harmonious compositions of all of these elements. Each of us is a body writhing in a net of needs, as well as a mind that has more subtle and vital needs than the body, and is driven by anxieties about the past and future to find answers to such questions as: "What am I? What is this world? What do life and death want from me? Who sent me to this world, and for what purpose? Where am I going, and what is the purpose of life? Who is my guide in this worldly journey?"

Moreover, each person is a creature of feelings that cannot be satisfied by the mind, and a creature of spirit, through which we acquire our essential human identity. Each individual is all of these. When a man or a woman, around whom all systems and efforts revolve, is considered and evaluated as a creature with all these aspects, and when all our needs are fulfilled, we will reach true happiness. At this point, true human progress and evolvement in relation to our essential being is only possible with education.

To comprehend education's significance, look at only one difference between us and animals. At the beginning of the journey from the world of spirits that extends into eternity at the earthly stage, we are weak, in need, and in the miserable position of waiting for everything from others.

Animals, however, come to this world or are sent as if they have gained perfection in another realm. Within 2 hours or 2 days or 2 months after their birth, they learn everything they need to know, their relation with the universe and the laws of life, and possess mastery. The strength to live and the ability to work that it takes us 20 years to acquire is attained by a sparrow or a bee in 20 days. More correctly, they are inspired with them. This means that an animal's essential duty is not to become perfect through learning and evolving by gaining knowledge or seeking help through showing its weakness. Its duty is to work according to its natural ability and thus actively serve its Creator.

On the other hand, we need to learn everything when we come into this world, for we are ignorant of the rules of life. In fact, in 20 years or perhaps throughout our whole life we still cannot fully learn the nature and meaning of life's rules and conditions, or of our relationship with the universe. We are sent here in a very weak and helpless form. For example, we can stand on their feet only after 1 or 2 years. In addition, it takes us almost our whole life to learn what is really in our interest and what is not. Only with the help of social life can we turn toward our interests and avoid danger.

This means that our essential duty, as a creation that has come to this passing guesthouse with a pure nature, is to reach stability and clarity in thought, imagination, and belief so that we can acquire a "second nature" and qualify to continue our life in "the next, much more elevated realms." In addition, by performing our duties as servants, we must activate our hearts, spirits, and all our innate faculties. By embracing our inner and outer worlds, where innumerable mysteries and puzzles reside, we must comprehend the secret of existence and thus rise to the rank of true humanity.

The religion–science conflict and its product, material-ism, have seen nature, like humanity, as an accumulation of material created only to fulfill bodily needs. As a result, we are experiencing a global environmental disaster.

Consider: A book is the material manifestation via words of its "spiritual" existence in the writer's mind. There is no conflict between these two ways of expressing the same truth and contents in two different "worlds." Similarly, a building has a spiritual existence in the archi-tect's mind, "destiny or pre-determination" in the form of a plan, and a building in the form of material existence. There is no conflict among three different worlds' ways of expressing the same meaning, content, and truth. Look-ing for conflict is nothing more than wasted effort.

Similarly, there can be no conflict among the Qur'an, the Divine Scripture (coming from God's Attribute of Speech), the universe (coming from His Attributes of Power and Will), and the sciences that examine them. The universe is a mighty Qur'an deriving from God's Attributes of Power and Will. In other words, if the term is proper, the universe is a large, created Qur'an. In return, being an expression of the universe's laws in a different form, the Qur'an is a universe that has been codified and put on paper. In its true meaning, religion does not oppose or limit science and scientific work.

Religion guides sciences, determines their real goal, and puts moral and universal human values before them as guidance. If this truth had been understood in the West, and if this relationship between religion and knowl-edge had been discovered, things would have been different. Science would not have brought more destruction than benefit, and it would not have opened the way for producing bombs and other lethal weapons.

Claims are made today that religion is divisive and opens the way to killing others. However, it is undeniable that religion, especially Islam, has not led to the last several centuries of merciless exploitation, especially the twentieth century's wars and revolutions that killed hundreds of millions of people and left behind even more homeless, widows, orphans, and wounded. Scientific materialism, a view of life and the world that has severed itself from religion, and a clash of interests caused such exploitation.

There is also the matter of environmental pollution, which is due to scientific materialism, a basic peculiarity of modern Western thought. Underlying pollution's global threat is the understanding, brought about by scientific unbelief, that nature is an accumulation of things that have no value other than meeting bodily needs. In fact, nature is much more than a heap of materiality or an accumulation of objects: It has a certain sacredness, for it is an arena in which God's Beautiful Names are displayed.

Nature is an exhibition of beauty and meaning that displays such profound and vast meanings in the form of trees taking root, flowers blossoming, fruit producing taste and aroma, rain, streams flowing, air breathed in and out, and soil acting as a wet-nurse to innumerable creatures. Thus, it makes a person's mind and heart like a honeycomb with the nectar that it presents to one's mind, which travels around like a bee, and to one's judgment and faculty of contemplation. Only the honey of faith, virtue, love of humanity and all creatures for the sake of the Creator, helping others, self-sacrifice to the extent of foregoing the passion of life to enable others to live, and service to all creation flow from this honeycomb.

As stated by Bediüzzaman [Said Nursi], there is an understanding of education that sees the illumination of the mind in science and knowledge, and the light of the heart in faith and virtue. This understanding, which makes the student soar in the skies of humanity with these two wings and seek God's approval through service to others, has many things to offer. It rescues science from materialism, from being a factor that is as harmful as it is beneficial from both material and spiritual perspectives, and from being a lethal weapon. Such an understanding, in Einstein's words, will not allow religion to remain crippled. Nor will it allow religion to be perceived as cut off from intelligence, life, and scientific truth and as a fanatical institution that builds walls between individuals and nations.

Serving Humanity through Education

Thanks to rapid developments in transportation and communication, the world has become a global village. Nations are exactly like next-door neighbors. However we must remember, especially in a world like this, that national existence can be ensured only by protecting each nation's specific characteristics. In a unified mosaic of nations and countries, those that cannot protect their unique characteristics, "patterns, and designs" will disappear. As with all other nations, our essential characteristics are religion and language, history and motherland. What Yahya Kemal, a famous Turkish poet and writer, expressed with deep longing in *The Districts without the Call to Prayer* was our culture and civilization that was brought from Islam and Central Asia and kneaded for centuries in Anatolia, Europe, and even Africa.

A related matter is the following. Among the people there is a saying: "A neighbor is in need of his/her neighbor's ashes." If you have no ashes needed by others, no one will attach any value to you. As mentioned above, we have more to give humanity than we have to take. Today voluntary or non-governmental organizations have founded companies and foundations and are serving others enthusiastically. The mass acceptance of the educational institutions that spread all over the world, despite the great financial difficulties they have faced, and their competing with and frequently surpassing their Western peers in a very short period of time, should be proof that what we have said cannot be denied.

As the Turkish people, we have accumulated many problems over the past several centuries. At their base lies our mistaken concentration on Islam's exterior and neglect of its inner pearl. Later on we began imitating others and surmised that there was a conflict between Islam and positive science. We did this despite the fact that the latter are no more than discoveries of Divine laws that manifest God's Attributes of Power and Will, and which are a different expression of the Qur'an coming from God's Attribute of Speech. This neglect, in turn, led to despotism in knowledge, thought, and administration; a hopelessness leading to disorder encompassing all individuals and institutions; confusion in our work; and not paying attention to the division of labor.

In short, our three greatest enemies are ignorance, poverty, and internal schism. Knowledge, work-capital, and unification can struggle against these. As ignorance is the most serious problem, we must oppose it with education, which always has been the most important way of serving our country. Now that we live in a global village, it is the best way to serve humanity and to establish dialogue with other civilizations.

But first of all, education is a humane service, for we were sent here to learn and be perfected through education. Saying: "The old state of affairs is impossible. Either a new state or annihilation," Bediüzzaman drew attention to solutions and the future. Saying that "controversial subjects shouldn't be discussed with Christian spiritual leaders," he opened dialogues with members of other religions. Like Jalal al-Din al-Rumi, who said: "One of my feet is in the center and the other is in seventy-two realms (people of all nations) like a compass," he drew a broad circle that encompasses all monotheists. Implying that the days of brute force are over, he said: "Victory with civilized persons is through persuasion," thus pointing out that dialogue, persuasion, and talk based on evidence are essential for those of us who seek to serve religion. By saying that "in the future humanity will turn toward knowledge and science, and in the future reason and word will govern," he encouraged knowledge and word. Finally, putting aside politics and direct political involvement, he drew the basic lines of true religious and national service in this age and in the future.

In the light of such principles, I encouraged people to serve the country in particular, and humanity in general, through education. I called them to help the state educate and raise people by opening schools. Ignorance is defeated through education; poverty through work and the possession of capital; and internal schism and separatism through unity, dialogue, and tolerance. However, as every problem in human life ultimately depends on human beings themselves, education is the most effective vehicle regardless of whether we have a paralyzed social and political system or one operating with a clockwork precision.

Schools

After the government allowed private schools, many people voluntarily chose to spend their wealth on serving the country, instead of passing on to the next world after a frivolous existence. In fact, they have done so with the enthusiasm of worship. It is impossible for me to know about all of the schools that have been opened both here and abroad. Since I only recommended and encouraged this, I do not even know the names of many of the companies that opened them or where the schools are located.

However, I have followed this matter to a certain extent in the press and in the series of articles by such worthy journalists as Ali Bayramoglu, Sahin Alpay, and Atilgan Bayar. Schools have been opened in places ranging from Azerbaijan to the Philippines and from St. Petersburg (the capital of Czarist Russia) and Moscow (the capital of communist Russia), and, with the help and reference of our Jewish fellow citizen and prominent businessman Üzeyir Garih, in Yakutsky. These schools have been opened in almost all countries, except for those like Iran that don't give their permission.

Writers and thinkers who have visited them state that these schools are financed by Turkish voluntary organizations. In many or all of them, student fees are an important part of this financing. Local administrators contribute sizable assistance by providing land, buildings, principals, and teachers when necessary. The teachers, who are dedicated to serving their country, nation, and humanity and have found the meaning of life to be in serving others, enthusiastically work for a small salary.

Initially, some of our foreign mission officials were hesitant to give their support, for they did not really understand what was going on. Today, however, most of them support the schools. In addition to Turkey's last two presidents, the late honorable Turgut Özal and the honorable Süleyman Demirel, as well as former Chairman of the Parliament Mustafa Kalemli and former Minister of Foreign Affairs Hikmet Çetin, showed their support by actually visiting the schools.

It is appropriate here to present Ali Bayramoglu's observations. A journalist who has visited many of these schools, he states:

> These schools don't give religious education or encompass educational activities with a religious environment, as is assumed. They have been established on the model of Anado-

lu high schools,[4] with superior technical equipment and laboratories. Lessons are given within the curriculum prepared by the Ministry of National Education. Religious subjects are not even taught. In fact, journalist Ali Bulaç, who visited these schools, related his impression that the toilets were purposely not kept sparkling clean to avoid the idea that praying might follow cleanliness. Activities take place within the framework of each country's current laws and educational philosophy. For example, in Uzbekistan, after students learn Turkish and English in the preparatory class, they study science in English from Turkish teachers and social subjects in Uzbek from Uzbek teachers. Giving religious knowledge or religious education is not the goal."

Local administrators are just as sensitive to secularism, or even more so, than the Turkish government. It has been explained by our enlightened journalists like Alpay, Bayar, and many others in a way similar to Bayramoglu's observations, that these countries do not feel the slightest concern for their future regarding these schools. In fact, speaking at the opening ceremonies for the school in Moscow, the Head of the Moscow National Education Office said: "There are two important events in Russia's recent history. One of these is Gagarin's landing on the moon. The other is the opening of a Turkish school here." He described this as an historic event.

For some, this life consists of the few days passed in this earthly guesthouse, and with the goal of completely fulfilling the ego's desires. Other people have different views, and so give life a different meaning. For me, this life consists of a few breaths on the journey that begins in the world of spirits and continues eternally either in Heaven or, God forbid, Hell.

This life is very important, for it shapes the afterlife. Given this, we should spend it in ways designed to earn eternal life and gain the Giver of Life's approval. This path passes through the inescapable dimension of servanthood to God by means of serving, first of all, our families, relatives, and neighbors, then our country and nation, and finally humanity and creation. This service is our right; conveying it to others is our responsibility.

Endnotes:

This article originally appeared in Unal Ali and Alphonse Williams, comps., *Fethullah Gülen: Advocate of Dialogue* (Fairfax, VA: The Fountain, 2000), 305-31.

1   Ibn Miskawayh (c.930-1030): Muslim moralist, philosopher and historian. His moral treatise *Tahdhib al-Akhlaq*, influenced by the Aristotelian concept of the mean, is considered one of the best statements of Islamic philosophy. His universal history *Kitab Tajarib al-Umam wa Ta'aqub al-Himam* (Eclipse of the 'Abbasid Caliphate), was noted for its use of all available sources and greatly stimulated the development of Islamic historiography.

2   A summary from Gülen's articles published in *Sizinti*, March 1981-June 1982, nos. 26-41.

3   This opposition was due to two factors: the Catholic Church refused to come to terms with new scientific discoveries and concepts, and the emerging new middle class wanted to be free of religion's disciplining rules.

4   Anadolu high schools is the term for the state-run schools in which scientific subjects are taught in English.

**What Others Say
about M. Fethullah Gülen**

Turkey Assails a Revered Islamic Moderate

Douglas Frantz

Onur Elgin, a Turkish teenager, has no doubts about why he spent his summer vacation studying physics. In fluent English, he explains that he wants to succeed for his school, his country and the world.

Onur's high school, Fatih College, is part of a prospering Islamic community associated with Fethullah Gülen, a 62-year-old religious leader who lives in Pennsylvania. In addition to hundreds of schools in Turkey, the Balkans and Central Asia, the loose-knit brotherhood runs a television channel, a radio station, an advertising agency, a daily newspaper and a bank, all pro-Islamic and all centered in Istanbul.

Though little known in the United States, for many years Mr. Gülen was an unofficial ambassador for Turkey who promoted a moderate brand of Islam. He preached tolerance, meeting with Pope John Paul II and other religious and political leaders, among them Turkey's prime ministers and presidents.

But this month, after a yearlong inquiry, a state security court issued an arrest warrant for Mr. Gülen. A prosecutor has accused him of inciting his followers to plot the overthrow of Turkey's secular government, a crime punishable by death. The authorities have not tried to extradite Mr. Gülen, but the warrant sent a chill through his circle of admirers and raised anxieties among liberals who are not associated with his movement.

At the same time, the government has been involved in a highly public dispute over its attempt to fire thousands of civil servants suspected of ties to pro-Islamic or separatist groups. Prime Minister Bulent Ecevit sought the authority for the dismissals through a governmental decree, but the president, Ahmet Necdet Sezer, has twice refused to sign the measure into law. Mr. Sezer argues that the authority can be created only by Parliament. The government agreed today to submit the matter to Parliament in the fall.

The deadlock has led to some calls for the resignation of Mr. Sezer, who took office in May. It has also contributed to the almost continuous tension between hard-line backers of the country's secular order and people who advocate more tolerance of religious views and free speech.

In a written response to questions from *The New York Times*, Mr. Gülen recently broke a year of public silence about the accusations against him. He described the charges as fabrications by a "marginal but influential group that wields considerable power in political circles."

He said he was not seeking to establish an Islamic regime but did support efforts to ensure that the government treated ethnic and ideological differences as a cultural mosaic, not a reason for discrimination.

"Standards of democracy and justice must be elevated to the level of our contemporaries in the West," said Mr. Gülen, who has been receiving medical care in the United States for the past year and said his health prevented his return to Turkey.

Turkey's military leaders have long regarded Mr. Gülen as a potential threat to the state. Those fears seemed confirmed a year ago when television stations broadcast excerpts from videocassettes in which he seemed to urge his followers to "patiently and secretly" infiltrate the government.

Mr. Gülen said his words had been taken out of context, and some altered. He said he had counseled patience to followers faced with corrupt civil servants and administrators intolerant of workers who were practicing Muslims.

"Statements and words were picked with tweezers and montaged to serve the purposes of whoever was behind this," he said.

Mr. Gülen's explanations are unlikely to satisfy the secular hard-liners who see themselves as the guardians of modern Turkey, which was founded in 1923 by Mustafa Kemal Ataturk. For them, the businesses and schools run by his followers sow the seeds of an Islamic regime.

Some moderate Turks see such Islamic-oriented schools and businesses as an attempt to fill a gap left by government policies and discrimination. A study by the private Turkish Economic and Social Studies Foundation found that these Islamic groups appeal not only to the poor but also to strict Muslims who often feel excluded from the mainstream.

The Gülen-oriented schools teach only government-approved religious instruction, in Turkish and English. Tuition payments are several thousand dollars a year, and students face rigorous academic challenges.

"Strategically speaking, the schools are something that should be supported by the state because you have a Turkish presence in these countries," said Ozdem Sanberk, director of the Economic and Social Studies Foundation.

At Fatih school outside Istanbul, the young Mr. Elgin, 16, has no intention of overthrowing the state. His sole goal right now is learning enough physics to compete on the Turkish national academic team.

Endnote:

This article originally appeared in *The New York Times*, August 25, 2000. Reprinted with permission.

True Muslims Cannot
Be Terrorists

I slam literally means "surrender." Islam is the religion of contentment, security and peace. These principles are so commonplace in a Muslim's life that when he stops to pray *salat* he cuts off all ties with the world, bows and prostrates before God and then he stands with hands clasped in respect. When he comes out of prayer, it is like starting a new life. He ends the prayer by greeting those to his left and right and wishing them health, security and peace, then goes and joins the other people.

Greeting others and wishing them peace are considered among the most auspicious acts that are done in Islam. Indeed, when Prophet Muhammad (pbuh) was asked, "What is the most auspicious act in Islam?" he replied, "Giving food to others and greeting all those you know and do not know."

Accusations of Terrorism

It is a great shame that Islam, which is based on those tenets, is seen by others to be the same as terrorism. This is a huge historical mistake because as we pointed out above, for a system based on peace and security to be as-

sociated with terrorism first and foremost shows that
those people know nothing of the spirit of Islam and are
unable to grasp it through their own souls. One should
seek Islam through its own sources and its own true representatives throughout history, and not through the actions of a tiny minority that misrepresent it. The truth is
that there is no harshness and bigotry in Islam. It is entire-
ly a religion of forgiveness and tolerance. Such pillars of
love and tolerance like Mawlana, Yunus Emre, Ahmed
Yesevi, Bediüzzaman and similar figures expressed this aspect of Islam most beautifully and went down in history
as examples of this affection and tolerance.

Jihad in Islam

Jihad is an element of Islam based on certain specific principles aimed at removing all the obstacles to the defense or
the exaltation of the name of God. We can cite numerous
examples throughout history in connection with this topic. As a nation we put up a sterling defense on many fronts
such as Canakkale and Trablusgarp. Had we not, were we
going to say to these enemies intent on occupying our
country, "You have come to make us civilized. That's good
of you. Welcome. Look, you've brought soldiers!" There
are always going to be battles, which are an inescapable
reality of humanity. However, the verses in the Koran revealed to Muhammad (pbuh) specifying conditions for
Jihad are misinterpreted by others to mean the main aim
of Islam. In essence, these people, who have failed to
grasp the true spirit of Islam, are unable to strike a balance
between the broad and finer points and this, when cou-

pled to the fact they are consumed with hatred, leads them to misinterpret Islam, whereas the breast of a genuine Muslim community is full of love and affection for all creation. A poet once wrote: Muhammad was begotten of affection; without Muhammad what comes of affection!

Love Binds Existence

Yes, Muhammad (pbuh) is a man of affection. He is also known as "Habibullah," which comes from the word "habib" which means "he who loves God and is loved by God." Mystics such as Imam Rabbani, Mevlana Halid and Shah Veliyullah Dehlevi say that the highest degree is that of love.

God created the whole of creation out of love and Islam has embroidered the delicate lacework of this love. In the words of another great mystic, love is the *raison d'être* for the existence of creation. Of course, in spite of all this, we cannot deny that Islam does have an element of violence in the name of deterrence. However, some people take these elements, which should be secondary, and consider them to be what Islam is all about, whereas Islam is peaceful. Once, a friend of mine who shared these sentiments told me, "You speak with everybody without imposing any restrictions. This in turn breaks the tension we have, whereas we have been taught that according to Islam we should show our hostility to certain people in the name of God." Actually, this thought stems from the incorrect interpretation of this idea. In Islam, everything that is created is to be loved in the name of God. What is to be hated and shown hostility are impure and immoral thoughts and feelings and blasphemy. God meant man as a kind creature (17:70) and one can say that everyone is blessed with that quality to varying extents. The Prophet of God (pbuh) was passing a Jewish funeral and he stopped to pay his respects. When reminded that the man being buried was a Jew, Muhammad replied, "He is still human though." He showed the value given to humanity in Islam.

Yes, this was the measure of our Prophet's respect for people. What lies behind certain Muslim people or institutions that misunderstand Islam getting involved in terrorist attacks that occur throughout the world should be sought not in Islam but within those people themselves, in their misinterpretations and in other factors. Just as Islam is not a religion of terrorism, any Muslim who correctly understands Islam cannot be thought of as a terrorist.

Given that there are bound to be exceptions, the interpretations of Islam by Turks are very positive. If we can spread the understanding of Islam held by the pillars of affection like Mawlana and Yunus Emre throughout the world, and if we can get their message of love, dialogue and tolerance to those people parched for this message, then people from all over the world will come running into the arms of this love, peace and tolerance we represent.

The tolerance of Islam is so vast that the Prophet (pbuh) specifically banned even the saying of things that would offend people. Despite all the self-sacrificing efforts by Muhammad, Abu Jahil failed to become a Muslim and died a wretch. In fact the name Jahil means ignorant. In fact, this ignorant and coarse man spent all his life as the enemy of the Prophet (pbuh) and his attitude has become second nature to Muslims. Saying that, shortly after the conquest of Makka Abu Jahil's Muslim son started saying things in council against his father and was reprimanded by the Prophet (pbuh) for doing so.

Respect for Mankind

In another *hadith* (story of the words and deeds of the Prophet [pbuh]), he said it was a great sin to swear at somebody's mother or father. They asked him if people ever swore at their in-laws. He replied that if someone swears at another's father or at another's mother, then he causes his own mother or father to be sworn at and is in effect guilty of swearing at them himself.

While the Prophet (pbuh) went out his way to show respect for others, the fact that today people are citing religion when being offensive to others means that they have not properly understood their Prophet. This is because there is no room for hate and hostility either in Islam or in the multicolored world of its envoy Muhammad (pbuh).

Servants of God

When we read the Koran, we see that it is based throughout on forgiveness and tolerance. In the passage "The House of Imran" in the Koran it reads: 'Those who spent benevolently in ease and straightness, and those who restrain their anger and pardon men; and God loves those who do good to others.' (3:133) Let us explain further. You encounter an incident that makes your blood boil; for example, people have sworn at and insulted you. As much as you can, you should behave indifferently and without reacting. The Koran describes how people of good morals should behave even at times when you just want to snap: "They're such magnanimous people that when they are confronted with events that would drive them crazy they swallow their anger like it was a thorn and they turn a blind eye to the faults of others." The Arabic words from this passage have much meaning. "Kezm" means swallowing what cannot be swallowed; while Kazim means someone who swallows his anger.

In another passage, God tells his followers: "And they who do not bear witness to what is false, and when they pass by what is vain, they pass by nobly" (25:71).

An Islamic Style

When we look at the exalted life of the Prophet (pbuh), we see that he practiced everything preached in the Koran. For example to someone who came and admitted adultery asking to be cleansed of his sins whatever the punishment may be, the Prophet (pbuh) said, "Go home, repent. There is no sin God does not forgive." Another hadith tells how a person accused another to the Prophet (pbuh) of stealing from him. Just when the penalty was about to be stated, the man turned and forgave the thief, to which Muhammad (pbuh) said, "Why didn't you forgive him in the first place?"

So, when all of these are examined in detail from their own sources, it will be seen that the style adopted by those who treat others with hatred and hostility, whose opposition to Muslims, Jews and Christians apart from themselves has been sharpened with anger and who smear them by calling them "infidel," is not in keeping with Islam at all. As we pointed out above, Islam is a religion of love and tolerance. Muslims are the bodyguards of love and affection, who shun all acts of terrorism and who have purged their bodies of all manner of hate and hostility.

Endnote:

This article originally appeared in *Turkish Daily News*, September 19, 2001, taken as it is from the book *Tolerance and Atmosphere of Dialogue in Fethullah Gülen's Writings and Sayings*. Reprinted with permission.

Gülen as Educator and Religious Teacher

Thomas Michel

I have come to know first the educational institutions conducted by participants of the movement led by Mr. Gülen. This has led me in turn to study his writings to discover the rationale that lies behind the educational venture that has ensued from the educational vision of Fethullah Gülen and his colleagues.

At the outset, it is necessary to be precise about the relationship of Mr. Gülen to the schools that are often loosely called "Gülen schools," or "schools of the Gülen movement." Mr. Gülen describes himself primarily as an educator. However, he is careful to distinguish between education and teaching. "Most human beings can be teachers," he states, "but the number of educators is severely limited."[1]

He has also tried to make clear that he has no schools of his own. "I'm tired of saying that I don't have any schools," he affirms with a bit of exasperation.[2] The schools have been established by individual agreements between the countries in which they are located and the educational companies founded for this purpose. Each school is an independently run institution, but most of the schools rely on the services of Turkish companies to provide educational supplies and human resources.

My first encounter with one of these schools dates back to 1995, in Zamboanga, on the southern Philippine island of Min-danao, when I learned that there was a "Turkish" school several miles outside the city. On approaching the school, the first thing that caught my attention was the large sign at the entrance to the property bearing the name: "The Philippine–Turkish School of Tolerance." This is a startling affirmation in Zambo-anga, a city almost equally 50% Christian and 50% Muslim, located in a region where for over 20 years various Moro [Muslim] separatist movements have been locked in an armed struggle against the military forces of the government of the Philippines. In a region where kidnapping is a frequent occurrence, along with guerrilla warfare, summary raids, arrests, disappearances, and killings by military and para-military forces, the school is offering Muslim and Christian Filipino children, along with an educational standard of high quality, a more positive way of living and relating to each other. My Jesuit colleagues and the lay professors at the Ateneo de Zamboanga confirm that from its beginning, the Philippine–Turkish School of Tolerance has maintained a deep level of contact and cooperation with Christian institutions of the region.

Since that time I have had occasion to visit other schools and discuss educational policy with the teaching and administrative staff. The strength of their programs in the sciences, informatics, and languages is shown in their repeated successes in academic olympiads. In a junior high school in Bishkek, I addressed a group of seventh-grade Kyrghyz children for about a half-hour. At the end of my talk, the teacher asked the students to identify those elements of pronunciation and vocabulary that showed that I was speaking an American rather than a British form of English, and to my amazement the children had no difficulty in doing so.

I had expected to find a more explicitly Islamic content to the curriculum and the physical environment, but this was not the case. When I asked about the surprising absence of what to me would have been an understandable part of a religiously-inspired educational project, I was told that because of the pluralist nature of the student bodies—Christian and Muslim in Zamboanga, and Buddhist and Hindu as well in Kyrghyz-stan—that what they sought to communicate were universal values such as honesty, hard work, harmony, and conscientious service rather than any confessional instruction.

These encounters led me to study the writings of Fethullah Gülen to ascertain the educational principles and motivation which undergird the schools and to try to find Gülen's own techniques that have made him into an educator capable of inspiring others with his vision.

The Educational Vision of Fethullah Gülen

In the decades since the establishment of the Turkish Republic, many Turkish Muslims have criticized the "modernization" program undertaken by the government for blindly adopting the best and worst of

European civilization. They have seen secularization as not merely an unintended by-product of the secularization process, but rather as the conscious result of an anti-religious bias. They contend that the unspoken presumption that underlay the modernizing reforms has been an ideological conviction that religion is an obstacle to progress and must be excluded from the public sphere of society, economics, and politics if the nation is to move forward. The battle lines drawn up during the decades since the establishment of the Republic, and reinforced by the mutually competitive systems of education, have made the religion–secularization debate in Turkey one in which every thinker is expected to declare their allegiance.

One of the reasons why, in my opinion, Fethullah Gülen has been often attacked by both "right" and "left," by "secular" and "religious" in Turkey is precisely because he has refused to take sides on an issue which he regards as a dead-end. He is instead offering a future-oriented approach by which he hopes to move beyond the ongoing debate. Gülen's solution is to affirm the intended goal of modernization enacted by the Turkish Republic, but to show that a truly effective process of modernization must include the development of the whole person. In educational terms, it must take the major concerns of the various existing streams of education and weave them into a new educational style which will respond to changing demands of today's world.

This is very different from reactionary projects which seek to revive or restore the past. Denying that the education offered in the schools associated with his name is an attempt to restore the Ottoman system or to reinstate the caliphate, Gülen repeatedly affirms that: "If there is no adaptation to new conditions, the result will be extinction."[3]

Despite the necessity of modernization, he holds, there are nevertheless risks involved in any radical break with the past. Cut off from traditional values, young people are in danger of being educated with no values at all beyond those of material success. Non-material values such as profundity of ideas, clarity of thought, depth of feeling, cultural appreciation, or interest in spirituality tend to be ignored in modern educational ventures which are largely aimed at mass-producing functionaries of a globalized market system.[4]

Such students might be adequately prepared to find jobs, but they will not have the necessary interior formation to achieve true human freedom. Leaders in both economic and political fields often favor and promote job-oriented, "value-free" education because it enables those with power to control the "trained but not educated" working cadres more easily. "Gülen asserts that if you wish to keep masses under control, simply starve them in the area of knowledge. They can escape such tyranny only through education. The road to social justice is paved with adequate, universal education, for only this will give people sufficient understanding and tolerance to respect the rights of others."[5] Thus, in Gülen's view, it is not only the establishment of justice which is hindered by the lack of well-rounded education, but also the recognition of human rights and attitudes of acceptance and tolerance toward others. If people are properly educated to think for themselves and to espouse the positive values of social justice, human rights and tolerance, they will be able to be agents of change to implement these beneficial goals.

If educational reform is to be accomplished, teacher training is a task that cannot be ignored. Gülen notes that "education is different from teaching. Most human beings can be teachers, but the number of educators is severely limited."[6] The difference between the two lies in that both teachers and educators impart information and teach skills, but the educator is one who has the ability to assist the students' personalities to emerge, who fosters thought and reflection, who builds character and enables the student to interiorize qualities of self-discipline, tolerance, and a sense of mission. He describes those who simply teach in order to receive a salary, with no interest in the character formation of the students as "the blind leading the blind."

The lack of coordination or integration among competing and mutually antagonistic educational systems gave rise to what Gülen calls "a bitter struggle that should never have taken place: science versus religion."[7] This false dichotomy, which during the 19-20th centuries exercised the energies of scholars, politicians, and religious leaders on both sides of the debate, resulted in a bifurcation of educational philosophies and methods. Modern secular educators saw religion as at best a useless expense of time and at worst an obstacle to progress. Among religious scholars, the debate led to a rejection of modernity and religion "as a political ideology rather than a religion in its true sense and function."[8]   He feels that through an educational process in which religious scholars have a sound formation in the sciences and scientists are exposed to religious and spiritual values, that the "long religion–science conflict will come to an end, or at least its absurdity will be acknowledged."[9]

For this to come about, he asserts that a new style of education is necessary, one "that will fuse religious and scientific knowledge together with morality and spirituality, to produce genuinely enlightened people with hearts illumined by religious sciences and spirituality, minds illuminated with positive sciences," people dedicated to living according to humane qualities and moral values, who are also "cognizant of the socio-economic and political conditions of their time."[10]

Several terms appear repeatedly in Gülen's writings on education and need to be clarified lest they cause misunderstanding. The first is that of *spirituality* and *spiritual values*. Some might read this as a code word for "religion" and employed to counteract prejudices towards religiosity in modern secular societies. However, it is clear that Gülen is using the term in a broader sense. For him, spirituality includes not only specifically religious teachings, but also ethics, logic, psychological health, and affective openness. Key terms in his writings are *compassion* and *tolerance*. It is the task of education to instill such "nonquantifiable" qualities in students, in addition to training in the "exact" disciplines.

Other terms used frequently by Gülen need to be examined. He often speaks of the need for *cultural*[11] and *traditional*[12] values. His call for the introduction of cultural and traditional values in education have been interpreted by critics as a reactionary call to return to pre-Republican Ottoman society. He has been accused of being an *irticaci*, which might be translated in the Turkish context as "reactionary" or even "fundamentalist." This is an accusation which he has always denied. In defense of his position, he states: "The word *irtica* means returning to the past or carrying the past to the present. I'm a person who's taken eternity as a goal, not only tomorrow. I'm thinking about our country's future and trying to do what I can about it. I've never had anything to do with taking my country backwards in any of my writings, spoken words or activities. But no one can label belief in God, worship, moral values and purporting matters unlimited by time as *irtica*."[13]

In proposing cultural and traditional values, he seems to regard Turkey's past as a long, slow accumulation of wisdom which still has much to teach modern people, and much in traditional wisdom is still quite relevant to the needs of today's societies. The past must not be discarded because of this collected wisdom. On the other hand, any attempts to reconstruct the past are both shortsighted and doomed to failure. One might say that while rejecting efforts to break with the past, Gülen equally rejects efforts to reestablish or recreate pre-modern society.

The tendency among some modern reformers to "break free of the shackles of the past" he regards as a mixed blessing. Those elements of the heritage that were oppressive, stagnant, or had lost their original purpose and inspiration no doubt have to be superseded, but other, liberating and humanizing elements must be reaffirmed if new generations are going to be able to build a better future. It is clear that his thinking is not limited by internal debates about political directions in Turkey, nor even the future of Islamic societies. His educational vision is one that embraces societies "throughout the world." He wants to form reformers, that is, those who, fortified with a value system that takes into account both the physical and non-material aspects of humankind. He states: "Those who want to reform the world must first reform themselves. In order to bring others to the path of traveling to a better world, they must purify their inner worlds of hatred, rancor, and jealousy, and adorn their outer world with all kinds of virtues. Those who are far removed from self-control and self-discipline, who have failed to refine their feelings, may seem attractive and insightful at first. However, they will not be able to inspire others in any permanent way and the sentiments they arouse will soon disappear."[14]

Gülen states: "A person is truly human who learns and teaches and inspires others. It is difficult to regard as fully human someone who is ignorant and has no desire to learn. It is also questionable whether a learned person who does not renew and reform oneself so as to set an example for others is fully human."

Fethullah Gülen as a Teacher of Islam

The focus of this paper has been on Fethullah Gülen as an educator. His role as religious scholar and teacher is a topic that deserves careful examination, as does the study of his religious thought as a modern interpreter of Islam. Such questions are outside the scope of this paper. However, a study of his educational vision would not be complete without a brief look at his writings on Islam.

Of Gülen's more than 30 books, some are compilations of talks and sermons which he delivered to students and worshipers. Others are responses to questions put to him at one time or another by students. They range from studies of the biography of the Prophet Muhammad, to a basic introduction to Sufism, to a treatment of questions traditionally raised in the science of *kalâm*, to elaborations of essential themes of Islamic faith. These studies are directed not toward specialists but at a more general audience of educated Muslims.

What can be said about Fethullah Gülen's personal approach to interpreting the Islamic sources and tradition? The first thing that strikes the reader is his emphasis on morality and moral virtue, which he appears to stress as more central to the religious élan inspired by the Qur'an than ritual practice. While affirming the need for ritual, Gülen regards ethical uprightness as lying at the heart of the religious impulse. "Morality," he states, "is the essence of religion and a most fundamental portion of the Divine Message. If being virtuous and having good morals is to be heroic — and it is — the greatest heroes are, first, the Prophets and, after them, those who follow them in sincerity and devotion. A true Muslim is one who practices a truly universal, therefore Muslim, morality." He buttresses his point by citing a hadith from Muhammad in which he states: "Islam consists in good morals; I have been sent to perfect and complete good morals."[15]

The various aspects of the Islamic way of life are all meant to work together to produce the honorable, ethically upright individual. In this broad sense of *islâm* or submission of one's life to God, it can be said that the schools established by the movement associated with the name of Fethullah Gülen have as their inspiration an ethical vision that is rooted in Islam but is not limited in its expression to members of the *umma*. When Gülen speaks of forming students "dedicated to living according to humane qualities and moral values," who "adorn their outer world with all kinds of virtues," he is proposing a kind of universal ethical code which he as a Muslim has learned from Islam. It is equally obvious that he does not consider the virtues, humane qualities and moral values to be the exclusive possession of Muslims, as non-Muslim students are welcome in the schools and no attempt is made to proselytize.

The religion of Islam is thus understood as a "way leading a person to perfection or enabling one to reacquire one's primordial angelic state."[16] If Islam is seen as a path to moral perfection, one must consider the development of *tasawwuf* as a natural and inevitable development within the Islamic tradition. Gülen suggests an ethical definition of Sufism as "the continuous striving to be rid of all kinds of bad maxims and evil conduct and acquiring virtues."[17] He praises the Sufis in Islamic history as being spiritual guides who have shown generations of Muslims how to follow this path to human perfection.

Such a positive reading of the mystical Sufi tradition has inevitably led to accusations of his having created within his movement a type of neo-Sufi *tarekat*. While denying that he has ever been a member of a *tarekat*, much less that he has set up his own quasi-Sufi order, Gülen asserts that to condemn Sufism, the spiritual dimension of Islam, is tantamount to opposing the Islamic faith itself. He states: "I have stated innumerable times that I'm not a member of a religious order. As a religion, Islam naturally emphasizes the spiritual realm. It takes the training of the ego as a basic principle. Asceticism, piety, kindness and sincerity are essential to it. In the history of Islam, the discipline that dwelt most on these matters was Sufism. Opposing this would be opposing the essence of Islam. But I repeat, just as I never joined a Sufi order, I have never had any relationship to one."[18]

Endnotes:

A summary of the paper presented by Dr. Thomas Michel, General Secretary of Vatican Secretariat for Interreligious Dialogue, in the "F. Gülen Symposium" (Georgetown University, April 2001). Reprinted with permission.

1 *Criteria or Lights of the Way* (Izmir: Kaynak, 1998), 1:36.
2 Lynn Emily Webb, *Fethullah Gulen: Is There More to Him Than Meets the Eye?*, 106.
3 Webb, *Fethullah Gulen*, 86.
4 *Towards the Lost Paradise*, 16.
5 "M. Fethullah Gulen: A Voice of Compassion, Love, Understanding and Dialogue," Introduction to M. Fethullah Gulen, "The Necessity of Interfaith Dialogue: A Muslim Approach," presented at the Parliament of the World's Religions, Cape Town, South Africa, Dec. 1-8, 1999.
6 *Criteria, or Lights of the Way*, 1:36.
7 "The Necessity of Interfaith Dialogue," 39.

8   Ibid., 20.

9   Ibid., 39.

10 Ibid.

11 Cf., "Little attention and importance is given to the teaching of cultural values, although it is more necessary to education. If one day we are able to ensure that it is given importance, then we shall have reached a major objective." *Criteria or Lights of the Way*, 1:35.

12 Cf. *Towards the Lost Paradise*, 16, and *Criteria or Lights of the Way*, 1:44-45.

13 Webb, *Fethullah Gulen*, 95.

14 "The Necessity of Interfaith Dialogue," 30.

15 *Towards the Lost Paradise*, 30.

16 *Prophet Muhammad: The Infinite Light*, 2:153-54.

17 *Key Concepts in the Practice of Sufism*, 1.

18 Webb, *Fethullah Gulen*, 102-3.

**Excerpts from Various
Interviews**

Islam Is Misunderstood[1]

We must review our understanding of Islam. As Muslims, we must ask ourselves why, in this world, others advance and we go backward? Taking the Qur'an and Sunna as our main sources and respecting the great people of the past, in the consciousness that we are all children of time, we must question the past and present. I'm looking for laborers of thought and researchers to establish the necessary balance between the unchanging and changing aspects of Islam and, considering such jurisprudential rules as abrogation, particularization, generalization, and restriction, can present Islam to the modern understanding. The first 5 centuries of Islam were the period when there were many such researchers and scholars. During this period there was a very broad freedom of thought. Only in such an atmosphere can great scholars and thinkers be raised.

There Is No Dogmatism in Islam[2]

Q: What's Islam's attitude toward dogmatism?

A: If dogmatism means to accept or copy something blindly without leaving room for free thought and use of mental faculties, there is no dogmatism in Islam. Especially under the conception of religion that has developed in the West, knowing and believing are considered as different things. In Islam, however, they complement each other. The Qur'an insists that everyone use his or her mental faculties (e.g., thinking, reasoning, reflecting, pondering, criticizing, evaluating, etc.).

Q: What about the Qur'anic verses that are decisive in canon law?

A: There are fixed, unchanging aspects of creation and life. As the "laws of nature" never change, as the essential aspects of humanity (e.g., its nature, basic needs, feelings, and so on) never change, a religion addressing humanity must have unchanging principles and perennial values. In addition, such moral standards as truthfulness, chastity, honesty, respect for elders (especially parents), compassion, love, and helpfulness are always universally accepted values. Likewise, refraining from alcohol, gambling, adultery and fornication, robbery, deception, and unjust ways of making a living are also universally accepted. Accepting and considering such standards and values while making laws is not dogmatism.

However, as in all other religion, Islam has experienced some dogmatist attitudes. For example, Zahirism began during the reign of 'Ali as a result of Kharijite extremism. They accepted verses with their external meaning only, and refused to consider such basic rules as abrogation, particularization, and generalization. In the beginning, it did not become a school of thought. However, people like Dawud al-Zahiri and Ibn al-Hazm established this as a system in Andalusia and published books on it. Later this school passed into the hands of some influential persons like Ibn al-Taymiyya, and influenced such scholars as Ibn al-Qayyim al-Jawzi-yya, Imam Dhahabi, and Ibn al-Kathir. It subsequently gave rise to Wahhabism. However, such people have always represented only a small minority.

Islam, Theocracy, and Tyranny[3]

Q: In Islam, is there despotism or theocracy as the media assert?

A: Some people, just as they can use everything for evil, can exploit Islam and use religion for despotic rule. But this doesn't mean that Islam has a despotic aspect. I think such a claim is due to not comprehending this matter correctly. Islam has nothing to do with theocracy, which is, in one respect, a system of government put forth by the church fathers' interpretation. In Islam there is no official clerical hierarchy, nor a clerical system.

Fundamentalism[4]

Fundamentalism means fanatical and dogmatic adherence to a belief. It has nothing to do with Islam, even though some people ascribe the Iranian and Saudi movements to fundamentalism. But this does not mean that Islam envisages fundamentalism. Iranian and Saudi versions are particular to themselves arising from the sect followed by each. The majority of Muslims do not accept either. It is a mistake to consider Islam as fundamentalism or Muslims as fundamentalists. The matter is locked into conceptual confusion. First this has to be clarified.

Women and Women's Rights[5]

Q: What are your thoughts about women's rights?

A: This is a very comprehensive subject. From one perspective it's open to debate. It's very difficult for me to summarize my thoughts on this kind of platform. In one sense we don't separate men and women. In one sense there are physical and psychological differences. In my opinion, women and men should be the two sides of truth, like the two faces of a coin. Man without woman, or woman without man, cannot be; they were created together. Even Heaven is a real Heaven when both are together. This is why Adam stayed there with his mate. Man and woman complement each other.

Our Prophet, the Qur'an, and Qur'anic teachings don't take men and women as separate creatures. I think the problem here is that people approach it from extremes and disturb the balance.

Q: Are there examples for the female role?

A: In the social atmosphere of Muslim societies where Islam is not "contaminated" with customs or un-Islamic traditions, Muslim women are full participants in daily life. For example, during the earliest period of Islam, 'A'isha, the Prophet's wife, led an army. She also was a religious scholar whose views everyone respected. Women prayed in mosques together with men. An old woman could oppose the Caliph in the mosque on a juridical matter. Even in the Ottoman period during the eighteenth century, the wife of an English ambassador highly praised the women and mentioned their roles in Muslim families and society with admiration.[6]

Individuals and Individual Human Rights[7]

We shouldn't fear or feel anxiety about individuals, their development, or their motivating other individuals, for the Qur'an sees each individual as a type as compared to other types. The important thing is the source of the emotions and thoughts that nurture them. When individuals attain a certain way of thinking and understanding and reach a certain horizon, they'll comprehend that it's necessary to live a social life. Developed persons will feel the need to be with others, understand that they shouldn't be alone, and that they shouldn't harm other members of the society.

Those individuals educated along these lines, who don't use their rights and freedoms to harm others but to consciously choose others' interests above their own, should be allowed to develop individually. Otherwise, there will be constant judgment and condemnation, oppression and being oppressed, cruelty and victims of cruelty. This is one dimension of the tragic tableau in Turkey today.

Humanism[8]

Q: What is Islam's perspective on humanism?
A: Love is one of today's most talked about and most needed issues. Actually love is a rose in our belief and a realm of the heart that never withers. Before everything else, just as God wove the universe like lace on the loom of love, in the bosom of existence the most magical and charming music is always love. The strongest relationship among individuals in the family, society, and nation

is that of love. Universal love shows itself throughout the existence of the cosmos through help and support for each particle.

This is so true that the most dominant factor in the spirit of existence is love. As an individual of the universal chorus, almost every creature behaves and performs with its own style the magical tune it has received from God in a love melody. However, this exchange of love from existence to humanity, and from one creature to another, takes place in a subconscious way, because Divine Will and Divine willing completely dominate creatures that have no will. From this perspective, people consciously participate in this symphony of love in existence, and developing the love in their true nature, they investigate the ways to demonstrate it in a human way. Therefore, without neglecting the love in their spirit and for the sake of the love in their own nature, every person should offer real help and support to others. They should protect the general harmony that has been put in their spirit, or in respect to the love that has been put into the spirit of existence as a natural law.

In the framework of Islam's universal principles, the consideration and idea of love is very balanced. Oppressors and aggressors are denied this love, because just as love and mercy shown to oppressors makes them more aggressive, it also encourages them to violate the rights of others. For this reason, mercy should not be shown to people who threaten universal love. Mercy shown to an oppressor is the most merciless act towards the oppressed. The Prophet said: "Help your brother whether he's an oppressor or victim. You can help an oppressor if he stops oppressing (others)." It is possible to show mercy to a tyrant if he stops acting unjustly.

Endnotes:
1   Hulusi Turgut, *Sabah*, Mar. 23-31, 1997.

2   Eyup Can, "Reaching to the Horizon with Fethullah Gülen," (trans.) *Zaman*, August 1995.

3   Eyup Can, "Reaching to the Horizon with Fethullah Gülen," (trans.) *Zaman*, August 1995.

4   Ibid.

5   Ertugrul Özkök, "Hocaefendi Speaks," (trans.) *Hurriyet*, Jan. 23-30, 1995.

6   Lady Mary Wortley Montague.

7   Nevval Sevindi, "Interview with Fethullah Gülen in New York," (trans.) *Yeni Yüzyil*, August 1997.

8   S. Camci and Dr. K. Unal, *Tolerance and Atmosphere of Dialogue in Fethullah Gülen's Writings and Sayings* (trans.) (Izmir: Merkur Yayinlari, 1999), 218-22.

"IN TRUE ISLAM, TERROR DOES NOT EXIST."

Interview by *Nuriye Akman*

Islamic community sat aside for years saying, "Islam does not accord with terror," paying only lip service to the prevention of terror. However, the September 11th incident occurred. In the aftermath, bombings took place in many countries, including Turkey. It was discovered that the perpetrators came from among us. Don't you think we (Muslims) should have been alarmed before anything else?

Today, at best we can say that Islam is not known at all. Muslims should say, "In true Islam, terror does not exist." In Islam, killing a human is an act that is equal in gravity to unbelief. No person can kill a human being. No one can touch an innocent person, even in time of war. No one can give a *fatwa* (a legal pronouncement in Islam) in this matter. No one can be a suicide bomber. No one can rush into crowds with bombs tied to his or her body. Regardless of the religion of these crowds, this is not religiously permissible. Even in the event of war-during which it is difficult to maintain balances-this is not permitted in Islam. Islam states; "Do not touch children or people who worship in churches." This has not only been said once, but has been repeated over and over throughout history. What Our Master, Prophet Muhammad, said, what Abu Bakr said, and what 'Umar said is the same as what, at later dates, Salahaddin Ayyubi, Alparslan, and Kılıçarslan also said. Later on, Sultan Mehmet II, the Conqueror, also said the same. Thus, the city of Constantinople, in which a disorderly hullabaloo reigned, became Istanbul. In this city the Greeks did not harm the Armenians, nor did the Armenians harm the Greeks. Nor did the Muslims harm any other people. A short time after the conquest of Constantinople, the people of the city hung a huge portrait of the Conqueror on the wall in the place of that of the Patriarchate. It is amazing that such behavior was displayed at that time. Then, history relates that the Sultan summoned the Patriarch and gave him the key to the city. Even today, the Patriarchate remembers him with respect. But today, Islam, as with every other subject, is not understood properly. Islam has always respected different ideas and this must be understood for it to be appreciated properly.

I regret to say that in the countries Muslims live, some religious leaders and immature Muslims have no other weapon to hand than their fundamentalist interpretation of Islam; they use this to engage people in struggles that serve their own purposes. In fact, Islam is a true faith, and it should be lived truly. On the way to attaining faith one can never use untrue methods. In Islam, just as a goal must be legitimate, so must all the means employed to reach that goal. From this perspective, one cannot achieve Heaven by murdering another person. A Muslim cannot say, "I will kill a person and then go to Heaven." God's approval cannot be won by killing people. One of the most important goals for a Muslim is to win the approval of God, another being making the name of Almighty God known to the universe.

Is this how their logic works, "war used to be fought on the fronts; but now, everywhere is a battleground"? Do they perceive it as a kind of war or jihad? Do they think that a gate to Paradise will be opened for them?

The rules of Islam are clear. Individuals cannot declare war. A group or an organization cannot declare war. War is declared by the state. War cannot be declared without a president or an army first saying that there is a war. Otherwise, it is an act of terror. In such a case war is entered into by gathering around oneself, forgive my language, a few bandits. Another person would gather some others around himself. If people were allowed to declare war individually then chaos would reign; because of such small differences a front could be formed even between sound-thinking people. Some people could say, "I declare war against such and such a person." A person who is tolerant to Christianity could be accused as follows: "This man, so and so, helps Christianity and weakens Islam. A war against him should be declared and he must be killed." The result would be that a war is declared. Fortunately, declaring war is not this easy. If the state does not declare a war, no one can wage war. Whoever does this, even if they are scholars whom I admire, does not create a real war; this is against the spirit of Islam. The rules of peace and war in Islam are clearly set out.

If it is against the spirit of Islam, then why is the Islamic world so?

In my opinion, an Islamic world does not really exist. There are places where Muslims live. They are more Muslims in some places and fewer in others. Islam has become a way of living, a culture; it is not being followed as a faith. There are Muslims who have restructured Islam in accordance with their thoughts. I do not refer to radical, extremist Muslims, but to ordinary Muslims who live Islam as it suits them. The prerequisite for Islam is that one should "really" believe, and live accordingly; Muslims must assume the responsibilities inherent in Islam. It cannot be said that any such societies with this concept and philosophy exist within Islamic geography. If we say that they exist, then we are slandering Islam. If we say that Islam does not exist, then we are slandering humans. I do not think Muslims will be able contribute much to the balance of the world in the near future. I do not see our administrators having this vision. The Islamic world is pretty ignorant, despite a measured enlightenment that is coming into being nowadays. We can observe this phenomenon during the hajj. We can see this displayed during conferences and panels. You can see this in their parliaments through television.

There is a serious inequality in the subject matter. They-these Muslims-cannot solve the problems of the world. Perhaps it could be achieved in the future.

You mean, then, that the term "Islamic World" should not be used?

There is no such a world. Today, there is an Islam of the individual. There are some Muslims in different places of the world. One by one, all have been separated from one another. I personally do not see anyone who is a perfect Muslim. If Muslims are not able to come into contact with one another and constitute a union, to work together to solve common problems, to interpret the universe, to understand it well, to consider the universe carefully according to the Qur'an, to interpret the future well, to generate projects for the future, to determine their place in the future, then I do not think we can talk about an Islamic world. Since there is no Islamic world, every one acts individually. It could even be said that there are some Muslims with their own personal truths. It cannot be claimed that there is an Islamic understanding which has been agreed upon, approved by qualified scholars, reliably based upon the Qur'an, and repeatedly tested. It could be said that a Muslim culture is dominant, rather than Islamic culture.

It has been so since the fifth century AH (eleventh century AD). This started with the Abbasid Era and with the appearance of the Seljuks. It increased after the conquest of Istanbul. In the periods that followed, doors to new interpretations were closed. Horizons of thought became narrowed. The breadth that was in the soul of Islam became narrowed. More unscrupulous people begun to be seen in the Islamic world; people who were touchy, who could not accept others, who could not open themselves to everyone. This narrowness was experienced in the dervish lodges, as well. It is sad that it was even experienced in the *madrasas* (schools of theology). And of course, all of these tenets and interpretations require revision and renovation by cultivated people in their fields.

It appears that al-Qaeda network has an extension in Turkey. You explained about the religious side of the matter. Are there also other dimensions to this?
One of the people whom I hate most in the world is [Osama] Bin Laden, because he has sullied the bright face of Islam. He has created a contaminated image. Even if we were to try our best to fix the terrible damage that has been done, it would take years to repair.

We speak about this perversion everywhere on many different platforms. We write books about it. We say, "this is not Islam." Bin Laden replaced Islamic logic with his own feelings and desires. He is a monster, as are the people around him. If there are other people similar to them anywhere, then they too, are nothing more than monsters.

We condemn this attitude of Laden. However, the only way to prevent this kind of deeds is that Muslims living in the countries seeming to be Islamic-and I stated earlier that I do not perceive an Islamic world, there are only countries in which Muslims live-will solve their own problems.

Should they think in a totally different way when electing their leaders? Or should they carry out fundamental reforms? For the growth of a well-developed younger generation, Muslims must work to solve their problems. Not only their problems in the issue of terror, an instrument that is certainly not approved of by God, but also those concerning drugs and the use of cigarettes, two more prohibitions made by God. Dissension, civil turmoil, never-ending poverty, the disgrace of being governed by others, and being insulted after having put up with government by foreign powers are all problems that could be added to the list.

As Mehmet Akif Ersoy said: slavery, a multitude of troubles, addiction, the acceptance of things out of habit, and derision are all commonplace. All of these are anathemas to God, and all of these have been placed primarily on our nation. Overcoming these, in my opinion, depends on being a just human being and a human being who is devoted to God.

These pro-terror people grew up among us in Muslim families. We thought they were "Muslims." What kind of a transformation have they undergone that they became terrorists? Aren't we all guilty?

It is our fault; it is the fault of the nation. It is the fault of education. A real Muslim, one who understands Islam in every aspect, cannot be a terrorist. It is hard for a person to remain a Muslim if he becomes involved in terrorism. Religion does not approve of the killing of people in order to attain a goal.

But of course, what efforts did we make to raise these people as perfect humans? With what kind of elements did we bind them? What kind of responsibility did we take in their upbringing so that now we should expect them not to engage in terror?

People can be protected against becoming involved in terrorism by means of some virtues originating in the Islamic faith, such as, fear of God, fear of the Day of Judgment, and fear of opposing the principles of religion. However, we have not established the required sensitivity on this issue. There have been some minor attempts to deal with this neglected subject to date. But, unfortunately there have been some obstacles put in the way, by our countrymen.

Some say the kind of activities that we need should not be allowed. That is, courses teaching culture and morality should be totally forbidden in educational institutions. At the same time we contend that every requirement of life should be met in schools. Health education should be provided, taught by doctors. Classes related to general life and life in the home should be comprehensively taught in schools.

People should be instructed in how to get along with their future spouses, and how to raise their children. But the issues do not stop here. Both Turkey and other countries that have a large Muslim population suffer from drug abuse, gambling, and corruption. There is almost no one left in Turkey whose name has not been involved in some type of scandal. There are some goals that were supposed to be reached that have been reached. Yet, there are many objectives that still cannot be reached. You cannot question anyone concerning this. You cannot call the people in charge to account. They are protected, sheltered, and thus they have been left alone.

These people are people who grew up among us. All of them are our children. Why have some of them become bad guys? Why were some raised as bullies? Why have some of them rebelled against human values? Why do they come to their own country and blow themselves up as suicide-bombers?

All these people were raised among us. Therefore, there must have been something wrong with their education. That is, the system must have some deficiencies, some weak points that need to be examined. These weak points need to be removed. In short, the raising of human beings was not given priority. In the meantime, some generations have been lost, destroyed, and wasted.

Dissatisfied youth has lost its spirituality. Some people take advantage of such people, giving them a couple of dollars, or turning them into robots. They have drugged them. This has become a topic on the agenda these days which can be read about in magazines. These young people were abused to an extent that they could be manipulated. They have been used as murderers on the pretext of some crazy ideals or goals and they have been made to kill people. Some evil-minded people have wanted to achieve certain goals by abusing these young people.

These people have been turned into robots. Once, many people were killed in Turkey. This group killed that person, another group killed another person. Everyone was involved in a bloody fight before the military came and intervened on March 12, 1971 and later on September 12, 1980. People were almost out for one another's blood. Everyone was killing one another.[1]

Some people were trying to reach a goal by killing others. Everybody was a terrorist. The people on that side were terrorists; the people on this side were terrorists. But, everybody was labeling the same action differently. One person would say, "I am doing this in the name of Islam." Another would say, "I am doing it for my land and people." A third would say, "I am fighting against capitalism and exploitation." These all were just words. The Qur'an talks about such "labels." They are things of no value. But people just kept on killing. Everyone was killing in the name of an ideal.

In the name of these bloody "ideals" many were killed. This was nothing less than terror. Everybody, not only Muslims, was making the same mistake. Since everyone did it, one after another, these killings came to be a goal that was "realizable." Killing became a habit. Everyone began to get used to killing, even though killing another person is a very evil action. Once, one of my dearest friends killed a snake. He was a theology graduate and he is now a preacher. As a reaction to this action, I did not talk to him for a month. I said: "That snake had a right to live in nature. What right did you have to kill it?"

But today the situation is such that if 10 or 20 people are killed, or if the numbers are not as high as was feared, then we say, "Oh, that's not so bad, not too many have died." This incredible violence has become acceptable by people at a horrible level. "It's good that the number of the death is only 20-30," we say. In short, society as a whole has come to accept this as part of our daily lives.

This situation could have been prevented by education. The laws and regulations of the government could have prevented this. Some marginal groups who are being shielded, and therefore who cannot be stopped, are exaggerating trivial matters, and making important matters insignificant. There is a remedy for this. The remedy is to teach the truth directly. It should be made clear that Muslims cannot be terrorists. Why should this be made clear? Because people must understand that if they do something evil, even if it is as tiny as an atom, they will pay for that both here and in the Hereafter.[2]

Yes, killing a human is a very significant thing. The Qur'an says that killing one person is the same as killing all people. Ibn Abbas said that a murderer will stay in Hell for eternity. This is the same punishment that is assigned to unbelievers. This means that a murderer is subjected to the same punishment as an unbeliever. In short, in Islam, in terms of the punishment to be dealt on the Day of Judgment, a murderer will be considered to be as low as someone who has rejected God and the Prophet (an atheist in other words). If this is a fundamental principle of religion, then it should be taught in education.

Endnotes:

This text has been excerpted from the interview Gülen gave to Nuriye Akman, published in *Zaman* between March 22-April 1, 2004.

1   Turkey has suffered three military coups in the second half of the twentieth century. The given dates are the second and third, which took place due to unrest in society.
2   The Qur'an 99:7-8.

Fethullah Gülen and Pope John Paul II

Fethullah Gülen and Patriarch Bartholomeos, the Ecumenical Patriarch of Orthodox Community

Fethullah Gülen and Turkey's Chief Rabbi David Aseo

Fethullah Gülen and Israel's Sephardic Head Rabbi Eliyahu
Bakshi Doron

Fethullah Gülen and Dale F. Eickelman, Professor of Anthropology
and Human Relations at America's Darmouth College

Fethullah Gülen and late Cardinal John O'Connor,
former Archbishop of New York

Fethullah Gülen and Bülent Ecevit, former Prime Minister of Turkey

Those who lead the way must set a good example for their followers. Just as they are imitated in their virtues and good morals, so do their bad and improper actions and attitudes leave indelible marks upon those who follow them.

M. Fethullah Gülen

Index